Modelling
Signal Boxes

FOR RAILWAY LAYOUTS

Modelling Signal Boxes

FOR RAILWAY LAYOUTS

TERRY BOOKER

THE CROWOOD PRESS

First published in 2017 by
The Crowood Press Ltd
Ramsbury, Marlborough
Wiltshire SN8 2HR

www.crowood.com

British Library Cataloguing-in-Publication Data
A catalogue record for this book is available from the British Library.

ISBN 978 1 78500 296 0

Disclaimer
The author and the publisher do not accept any responsibility in
any manner whatsoever for any error or omission, or any loss,
damage, injury, adverse outcome, or liability of any kind incurred
as a result of the use of any of the information contained in this
book, or reliance upon it. If in doubt about any aspect of railway
modelling skills and techniques, readers are advised to seek
professional advice.

Designed and typeset by Guy Croton
Publishing Services, Tonbridge, Kent

Printed and bound in India by Parksons Graphics

CONTENTS

PREFACE

What lies ahead in this, my third book for The Crowood Press? Like the previous titles, it is an attempt to help readers, irrespective of their level of experience, to get a better understanding of the steam era and also to make the most of their modelling skills. The subject of 'signal boxes and signalling' is a vast one, with thousands of boxes controlling millions of points and signals and now, with the rapid development of computers and their associated technologies, a seemingly endless supply of new kits and modellers' aids. My main objective, therefore, is to cover as much as I can and hope that not too much more happens between the text leaving my keyboard and the finished publication reaching your bookshelf.

ACKNOWLEDGEMENTS

After more than half a century of modelling and 'linesiding', I owe a mention to so many individuals and organizations that it would need another complete chapter to thank them all properly for their contributions. Top of the list, however, must be my immediate family. For my early endeavours, my thanks go to my late parents for their encouragement and boundless generosity. Even in the bleak Austerity Years, when it was never easy to find two pennies to rub together, there was always something to help me on my way. For the last fifty years, my long-suffering better half has put up with an ever-expanding tide of model-making paraphernalia, which frequently overflows from the confines of the loft to the comfort of the lounge. Joan now not only tolerates the modelling and the annual pursuits of steam abroad, but also has the added burden of an author who is often locked away in the study. Thanks, too, for my sons, who treat me as a geriatric Peter Pan, 'the boy who never grew up', and give me trains not ties at Christmas.

My thanks also go to the many companies and individuals who have helped with the book by generously supplying samples or offering sound advice.

INTRODUCTION

Most modellers, whatever their age and their chosen gauge, will always remember their first train set and their first signal box. For me, that entails a step back in time of around seven decades, to the darkness of a winter's evening, in the dusty and dimly lit surroundings of my father's newly rented forge and workshop. It was no secret that the approach of my seventh birthday and of Christmas would soon be rewarded with some second-hand Hornby clockwork trains. Dad was making a signal box and, if I was really good, I had been promised a station too. As with everything my father did, it would be sturdy enough to withstand another war, never mind the accidental demolition efforts of a seven-year- old. I perched on his tool-strewn work-bench and watched him mark out and cut a sheet of hardboard. The still unfamiliar smell of the workshop was made up of wafts of Old Holborn tobacco from Dad's ever-present roll-up, and the pungent aroma from a large tin of ancient wood-glue that was slowly melting on the glowing embers of the forge. With the careful assembly of the half-dozen bits of hardboard, Hey Presto!, my signal box was born.

Of course I wanted to take it back up the village there and then, but the glue had to dry and it was already well past my bedtime. Sure enough, on Christmas morning there it was, together with the station, smart in its coat of brick-red paint with silver windows and ready to control its single signal to permit the 0-4-0 LNER tank and two coaches to hurtle past at speeds even 'Mallard' could not match. True to form, those two simple structures would last throughout the innocent years of my gauge '0' adventures, until they were sold in order to fund the beginnings of grown-up adventures with Hornby Dublo 3-rail.

Hand-operated point lever at Knighton Yard on 'Wessex Lines'.

Scratch-built Sykes banner repeater for the starting signals further along the platform at Sherborne Abbas.

A Standard 4-6-0 on the 'up oil', passing Knighton Yard box. It is surprising what a difference a coat or two of gloss varnish makes to an r-t-r engine.

It was not that many months later that I began my life-long enthusiasm for the steam railway. Challow station, halfway between Didcot and Swindon on Brunel's 'billiard table', was less than two downhill miles from home and in those distant days I was free to roam more or less as I pleased. My first real bike (also made by Dad!) could get me there in under half an hour, although it took somewhat longer coming back up to the village. At first I knew nothing about what to do in this strange world of 'trainspotting', but a few older boys instructed me in the practice of writing down the numbers in my newly acquired notebook. They went on to explain that the gleeful shouts of 'cop' did not imply some special type of train, but merely meant an engine that they had not seen before. The innocence of youth!

As the years rolled by the older ones drifted away, but I continued my journeys and soon invested my pocket money in the brown-covered Western Region Ian Allen ABC, and a new-fangled 'biro' to underline those cops. New-found school friends became occasional companions, but my visits tended to be solitary expeditions -- I travelled alone as far as Oxford, Swindon, Reading and Basingstoke, even before I had become one of those new so-called 'teenagers'.

However, as far as Challow was concerned, I found myself at an advantage; especially in the winter. Despite being well into his forties, Dad was still a regular on the village football and cricket teams, as was a certain Ken Rowland, whose day job just happened to be as one of the signalmen at Challow station. Whether out of friendship for my dad or pity for a forlorn and freezing schoolboy, the signal-box window would often slide back and I would be waved to come round. Having strategically placed myself in full view on the 'up' side, I would dash back over the road bridge, dump the bike (dad-built Mk2!), scramble over the fence to the meadow, run the hundred yards along to the back of the box, cross the fence again, remove the muddy wellies and climb the stairs to the highly polished warmth of the Challow signal box.

I cannot lay claim to having learned anything useful from those visits. For a start, I was far more concerned with the trains themselves than with what went on in the box, and Ken was far too preoccupied with the workings of this busy mainline post to spend time explaining the procedures to me. That said, the atmosphere of the place does remain a very vivid memory and is one that is always evoked with every signalman's autobiography that I read. Their jobs not only carried tremendous responsibility, but also entailed a great deal of autonomy. A team of conscientious and experienced signalmen working adjacent boxes could make all the difference to the smooth running of their stretch of railway. They and they alone would have to decide whether a late-running service should be put into the loop, and delayed still longer, in order to allow a following train to overtake and therefore keep to its schedule. A few quick phone calls would agree the proposals, the respective signals would be pulled off and the appropriate bell codes exchanged. The important train registers would then be written up and would eventually arrive at control. Of course, that wide-eyed twelve-year-old was largely unaware of all this, but, even on a normal day, any brief intervals of calm were all too quickly replaced by periods of seemingly frantic activity.

From memory I recall that Challow had around fifty levers, considerably more than the tiny box at Circourt Crossing (known as 'Sirkit' to us Berkshire boys), just over a mile away on the 'up' (Didcot) side. Uffington was the next box on its 'down' (Swindon) side and that was more comparable in size and was well out of sight as the line curved gracefully northwards. Challow's levers controlled the signal arms on the up-fast and down-fast, for the up and down relief lines to the east and for the platform loops, as well as for over a score of points, most of which were interlocked. Challow goods yard was also quite large and certainly more complex than those at its neighbouring stations. No wonder Ken Rowland was slim and fit -- he might well have as many as seven or eight trains in his block at any one time. Of one thing I am certain, even after all this time: signal boxes were not only the cleanest places on the entire railway, they were also the busiest.

Getting back to modelling, it was not long before my 3-rail left its semi-permanent home on our table-tennis top (built by Dad) and migrated to an 8 x 6ft garden shed (also built by Dad!). Now it was my turn to build something other than balsa-wood gliders, although that particular wood would still come in handy to reinforce the Bilteezi Country Station and Signal Box. There was almost nothing in the way of model-making equipment available in those days, so the kits were assembled using kitchen scissors, spent

Snow-clad Winterbourne on 'Wessex Lines'. One hundred per cent Bilteezi and built way back in the early 1970s, it has seen four reincarnations and a 100-mile house move. These kits are really admirable.

razor blades, Seccotine and balsa cement. None the less, although they were a far cry from today's offerings, I still considered them to be more realistic than the comparatively expensive Hornby Dublo models. Surprisingly, they also turned out to be pretty resilient and weathered many a cold, wet winter and scorching July day. Perhaps it will come as no surprise that I have included Bilteezi in the chapters that follow; it is the least I can do for a range of kits that have been continuously on the market for nearly seventy years.

For me (and many others, I suspect), there was no smooth transition from Dublo to 4mm scale modelling. A-levels, then a job and other social pursuits took precedence over playing trains, and almost a decade had passed before I gave another thought to railways, large or small. Even then, I came back to the hobby almost by accident. As the Saturday duty rep on the Oxford Mail, I was impatiently listening for the presses to roll with the lunch-time edition, waiting to be allowed to head home, when I spotted the headline: 'Last Steam Train from Oxford'. In my absence, someone had stolen 'my' railway and I realized to my dismay that everything I had once known had seemingly gone for ever. An hour later I left Woolworths

'Danger! Author at work…'

Pendon Museum in Oxfordshire is the zenith of the art of the card scratch-builder: the Parsons Tunnel box on their Devon coastal stretch.
ANDY YORK, COURTESY PENDON MUSEUM

clutching an Airfix Prairie Tank and two mineral wagons and after that weekend I was hooked. From this point, my military and aviation modelling would have to take a back seat. The long packed-away Dublo was sold (except for an 0-6-2 tank, kept out of pure sentiment) and a shelf in my flat soon boasted some 2-rail track, some more Airfix wagons and, of course, the Airfix signal box.

I had a lot of catching-up to do. It was apparent that, as the real steam railway had virtually disappeared, so the model railway world seemed destined to fill the void. The three monthly magazines, *Railway Modeller*, *Model Railway Constructor* and *Model Railway News*, offered all sorts of inspirational layouts, and were packed with advertisements for a huge range of items (if only the weekly wage packet would stretch that far). There were few, if any, proper books on modelling but at least Oxford's well-stocked library had copies of the works of Edward Beale and John Ahern. Even if I was not in a position to carry out a lot of construction, I could indulge in plenty of day-dreaming and scribbling; I would like to dignify it by calling it 'layout planning', but I have to admit it was not in that league. I did come up with two philosophies in those far-off days, however, both of which have stood the test of time. First, my goal would be to create systems that went somewhere; the single-station shunting plank was not for me. Second, I would write things down and plan every layout like a business model, not simply 'model a model'.

Soon after, I had the good fortune to be offered a promotion within my newspaper group and found myself living in an eighteenth-century cottage in Shap, with my wife and two young sons. It was not long before the small dining room was crammed with some dodgy carpentry and my first attempt at a railway that went somewhere. Actually, it went only rarely, as my track-laying and my electrics were of a similar standard to my woodwork. Even if the correct ways still eluded me, I did at least learn how not to do things, and, thanks to a gradually growing library and regular visits to the shows in York, Manchester, Leeds, Liverpool and Glasgow, my reserves of knowledge and stock began to expand. This was the early 1970s, and the hobby itself was only just getting into its stride. 'Stuff' was still hard to find (as was the cash to buy it), so, like most of that generation, I began to grapple with kit-bashing, conversions and refurbishing second-hand stock. It was a pleasurable pastime and the art of 'make do and mend' came quite naturally to this war baby.

Those formative years have continued to stand me in good stead over the years. I still derive enormous satisfaction from kit-building and kit-bashing, from scratch-building, from trying to re-create the railways I once knew, and from rescuing models. I take pride in the fact that nothing on my layouts is ever left in its straight-from-the-box condition. Anyone can own a superb model railway. Today's high standards of manufacture, together with reams of useful information, mean that a modeller's aspirations are limited only by the size of his or her bank balance. However, mere ownership does not necessarily imply satisfaction. I believe firmly that putting your skills to the test and making things for yourself will help you get the most out of this great hobby. Even the simple exercise of building a kit as per the instructions is more rewarding than buying a similar item off the shelf. However, when you take things a step further, and 'bash' or customize that kit into something closer to your ideal, you will have begun your transformation from model-railway owner to proper railway-modeller.

Clearly, railway modelling is alive and well, and this is evidenced by bookshops and magazine sellers offering a wide range of prototype and modelling titles, and by the vigorous discussions on various forums. Some of the information out there,

however, is slightly disturbing for the older modeller. Many of the magazines and newer 'bookzines' seem to imply that modelling is simple, and that all problems may be easily resolved. Perhaps this has to do with the modern concern with instant gratification? It certainly does no favours for the newer modeller, or, I suspect, for the longer-term future of the hobby. Any experienced modeller will affirm that the best results come with practice and persistence. Persuading a novice into believing that overnight success is achievable is likely to lead to disappointment, dissatisfaction and the premature abandonment of the hobby.

Even after a half-century of modelling, I still make mistakes and my carefully prepared plans often go awry. The work in this book has been written up and photographed as it happened -- no glossy studio shots, no tailor-made facilities and no resorting to 'Here's one we made earlier'! My aim is to present a relaxed tutorial in a domestic setting that will be familiar to most modellers.

My rendition of the once-familiar installations at Salisbury Tunnel Junction.

A scratch-built model of Dainton signal box, based on a handful of photographs and boasting a detailed interior.

Built for the book, this Metcalfe box is posed at Knighton Yard on 'Wessex Lines'; see Chapter 3 for a full description of its assembly.

The book will take a look at just a few of the 10,000 or more signal boxes inherited by British Railways in January 1948. As well as controlling almost every mile of track from Land's End to John o'Groats, they were also the highly polished homes of the small army of experienced signalmen who operated them. It is a happy coincidence for modellers that there was no such thing as the 'standard' signal box; it is difficult to claim that no two were ever alike, but their variety was almost infinite. At the dawn of BR there were still survivors from the original independent railways, based on different designs built by numerous contractors. The 'standard' types favoured by the larger

pre-grouping companies remained plentiful, alongside the slightly more recent house styles imposed by the Big Four. Most BR regions also had examples of wartime and post-war additions. If there was an infinite number of styles, then this was certainly matched by an infinite number of sizes; signal boxes really did range from a small shed covering four or five levers at a branch terminus to major installations with well over 150 levers at busy mainline junction stations.

The book will take a fairly broad view of the infrastructure and interior of the boxes, and will also spend some time looking at signals and signalling, a poorly modelled feature on too many otherwise excellent

Another of my scratch-built models, East Ilsley box takes a 'holiday' from its home on the exhibition modules to signal the Castle hauled 'up' Devonian.

layouts. When it comes to the modelling itself, there are many options currently available and the information will help you identify the ones best suited to your existing or planned layout; there are plenty to choose from, with new kits and off-the-shelf versions coming on to the market almost every month. Needless to say, despite this wide choice, many modellers will still want something perhaps slightly different or maybe they will want to re-create an exact replica of a particular example. That of course means venturing into customizing (also known as 'kit-bashing'), and ultimately into scratch-building, still making best use of any appropriate modellers' aids and accessories.

While on the subject of modelling an exact prototype, if your chosen box is on the real railway rather than on a preserved line, you would be well advised to photograph and measure it now. The last phase of bringing our much-loved Victorian signalling into line with the twenty-first century is well under way, and these once-familiar sights and installations are

disappearing at an alarming rate. I discovered this to my cost, when I considering illustrating the former LSWR/SR boxes at Hamworthy Junction, Wool and Poole in this book. In the week or so that elapsed before I was able to make the trip to photograph them, they had all been demolished! So do not delay: even if your model is only on a long-term wish list, make sure you capture that vital detail before it is turned into a pile of rubble.

As well as describing the step-by-step assembly of several types of kit, including laser-cut and downloads (together with occasional advice on how to improve them), the book will also visit a couple of popular tourist lines for scratch-builds. A visit to my 'Wessex Lines' loft layout will show other examples in their model environment and their temporary replacement with our project versions.

It is now time to 'set-the-road', pull off the 'starter' and tap 'train-leaving-section' to the next box. The journey starts here.

CHAPTER ONE

CHOOSING THE RIGHT BOX

THE STEAM ERA

It may seem a little odd to describe signal boxes as belonging to any particular period. They were, after all, around from the earliest days of the railways and are still lingering more than a century and a half later. But it is necessary to draw a line somewhere and the phrase 'steam era' manages to encompass around 100 years of railway history, from the colourful pre-grouping companies, through the decades of the 'Big Four' to the rather less colourful and rusty demise of steam under British Railways. The traditional signal boxes survived throughout that period and did so with very little change to their number, their role or their appearance. They did receive more than one lick of paint in that time – some of the older ones

probably had an inch of the stuff before finally succumbing to the pace of change. Since most modellers, and indeed most manufacturers, seem to concentrate their activities on the years between the late 1930s and the mid-1960s, it makes sense to follow their example. (I apologize to the 'pre-groupers' and the 'modern image' modellers, but even for your eras, your signal box will still only need that aforementioned lick of paint. And the out-of-use boarded-up windows would bring you right up to date.)

The illustrations here feature period black and white images, contemporary photographs and even some kit and scratch-built examples. Mainly, they have been chosen to give just a glimpse of the variety of sizes, styles, materials and designs that might be suitable for even the smallest of layouts.

The small ground-level signal box at the end of the former Lambourn Valley Railway is a sort of half-way house between a covered ground frame and a 'proper' box. AUSTIN ATTEWELL

Another ground-level example, which combines the all-timber construction with a hipped roof. The emerging signal wires and point-rodding are clearly shown. The rather sparse, but not unattractive, passenger facilities are quite sufficient for this wayside halt.
AUSTIN ATTEWELL

A FEW BASICS

The signal box is ubiquitous – there are 10,000 of them – and probably the simplest of any of the buildings on the railways, real or model. The descriptions that follow may all be preceded by 'as a general rule'. There will always be exceptions, but there is neither time nor space to cover every variation. Suffice it to say that the signal box is a four-sided rectangular structure, usually with two floors and either a hipped or ridged roof – a box with a lid. Some were square but more often they were oblong, with the longer side facing the track. The ground floor, often known as the locking room, contained the working machinery, which conveyed the movement of the upstairs levers to the signal wires and point-rodding outside. This lower floor had no more than a few windows and usually a single doorway, which also gave access to an internal staircase on certain types of box. The upper or operating floor, where it all happened, housed the lever frame itself and the requisite number and type of levers. Communication with the adjacent boxes was set out on a long instrument shelf positioned above the levers. Above this was a large panel representing the section controlled by

the box and showing its status at any given moment. This was the signal box 'diagram'.

In addition to this there would be all the paraphernalia associated with a busy working environment and its administrative and personnel needs. Depending upon the size and complexity of the box, there might be a stove, chair(s), desk(s), cupboard(s),

Another platform-based box, this time at St Columb Road – a very attractive little design and an ideal project for a first scratch-build.
AUSTIN ATTEWELL

notice-board(s) and telephones. There would also be limited domestic facilities, adequate for the number of staff on duty and the number of shifts operated. The toilet might be found downstairs, either in the locking room or in an outside lean-to. The operating floor would be as fully glazed as possible, to give clear views up and down the line.

SITING THE SIGNAL BOX

Those signal boxes with external access would have a flight of steps leading to a veranda or balcony. The steps could run at right-angles to the building or be built against the wall. The actual entrance to the operating floor could be via small lobby or direct from the veranda; and the veranda itself could be confined to just the access area or run around the front of the box. One point that is worth highlighting is the orientation of the structure. As a general rule, the entrance, whether at ground level or via the steps, would face towards the main station buildings. Unlike the model kits, this meant that any 'standard' designs could be constructed with the railway equivalent of left- or right-hand drive! As

to the question of which side of the line the box should be located, there is little consistency. While it is true that there are certain stretches of mainline where there is a level of conformity, there will always be at least one box that is on the other side. As a result, the modeller is free to site a box where it looks best, as long as that location still fulfils the operating requirements of the miniature signalman – most obviously in respect of its apparent sight-lines. Almost invariably, however, modellers will have their signal box facing the viewer.

EXPLORING OPTIONS

At its simplest, choosing a signal box for a layout need be no more time-consuming than trawling through the adverts, spending a few minutes in the local model shop, and purchasing a kit or a ready-to-site example to place beside the track. However, there are many more options than that. There are a number of factors to take into consideration when making your choice, and it is a sound idea to put pen to paper at this stage and list all the key points, which can then be marshalled into some order of priority.

Lostwithiel (GWR/ BRw) is surely a classic for the space-starved modeller? It comprises a large signal box built into the platform end, controlling a level-crossing, and a carriage bay and loco facilities immediately behind.
AUSTIN ATTEWELL

All typically GWR, but, as it is located on the platform, the usual locking-room windows have been omitted, probably for security reasons. AUSTIN ATTEWELL

Mortimer, between Reading and Basingstoke, is another standard GWR design with older-pattern windows. Those elegant spiked finials are definitely not standard, though. AUSTIN ATTEWELL

CREATING A SPECIFICATION

In order to illustrate this task, some broad assumptions need to be agreed: either the layout has already been built or the planning and back story are well advanced; the area and the era have been decided; the company or region that will operate the box has been identified; the probable location for the box and its likely size are also known; and, finally, the budget, in terms of money or time, or both, has been set. Now you can start your list.

The list might be presented as follows (or scribbled down as an accompaniment to the layout plan):

Geographic area: Yorkshire, secondary mainline, 'up' and 'down' through roads and passing loops, rural location
Company: NER/LNER/BR(NE)
Site size: 6in (150mm) by 4in (100mm)
Budget: cash £15 to £20, build time two weeks incl. interior
Desirables: card kit (customized kit?); similar to block-posts on Scarborough route; LNER or contractor built; approx. 20 levers; BR(E) colour-scheme period 1950-ish; make it higher to give better view over an adjacent road bridge? May

need different brick paper(s)?, add an interior with wires and rodding on the outside.

SPOILT FOR CHOICE?

You can do your research online or go window-shopping through the ads pages of the magazines, or look through albums for inspiration. In this case, the online option produced four possible examples, all within budget and some even allowing the additional cost of the point-rodding and interior-detailing kits.

For those modellers who are in a hurry and are prepared to push the budget, or perhaps dispense with the interior-detailing set(s), Hornby's larger 'Skaledale' box seems pretty much tailor-made for the job. It appears to be an accurately dimensioned and nicely finished version of a typical box found in the chosen area and it falls within the allocated footprint. However, it would not do to ignore the example in the Wills Scenics range. This is a slightly larger box and is modelled on one of the many versions built by contractors Saxby and Farmer. They were responsible for the signalling on several of the pre-grouping systems. This box could sit quite happily in this planned setting. It is a plastic kit, which is why it has been considered along with the previous item;

Barge-boards were much less common on the old GWR, but this may well be a contractor-built box with pre-grouping origins. AUSTIN ATTEWELL

when painted in the appropriate regional colours, the visual difference between them would be minimal.

In terms of card kits, the original Prototype (currently discontinued, but sometimes available via Freestone Models) would probably be my favourite. In this instance, these kits have no competitors. They are always accurate, well thought out, nicely finished and a pleasure to assemble. The box selected represents the one at Stamford and its footprint of roughly 140 x 90mm neatly fits the intended site. The downsides are that it does look more LNER than NER in its origins and it does tend to drift in and out of availability.

Moving on to the download kits, Smart Models have the edge, with their version of the Low Gates (Northallerton) signal box. This is more than appropriate in terms of geography, and, priced at just £3.99 with free repeats, it leaves plenty of budget to cover the requisite interior and rodding. The footprint is also commendably close to the brief, at 140mm by 110mm. It is also architecturally interesting in that it is a local BR design dating from the early 1950s and, if that were not enough, it also controlled a capstan-operated level-crossing.

Luxulyan is a typical GWR timber-built box, but with a hipped roof. Note the attractive (standard) corbels, the ventilators and the token apparatus. AUSTIN ATTEWELL

This former LSWR/SR box, now out of use, still stands at Wareham.

The original signal box at Swanage had to be replaced and re-sited, but now looks very much part of the landscape.

The signal box at Corfe Castle is an enthusiast-built replica of the original.

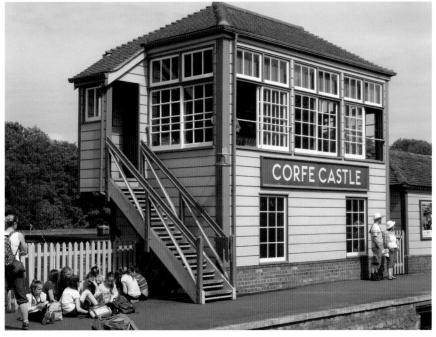

It is easy to see how wide the range of options is, even when starting with a relatively tight brief. There can be very few instances where the modeller is not given the choice of at least plastic or card construction; of ready-to-site or kit-build; or of something from the variety of downloads. Finally, if all else fails, the ever-increasing supply of modellers' aids makes scratch-building and kit-bashing into somewhat easier projects.

SIZING

The above example is pretty straightforward and it will certainly not match the aspirations of most modellers. However, there are some basic considerations that will apply in almost every decision-making exercise. The most basic of these is probably the actual size of the box; the design, style and regional identity can invariably be tweaked on the modelling bench.

As a general rule, the size of the box will be governed by the size of the lever frame and that, of course, is determined by the number of signal arms, points, interlocking levers, detonators and crossing-gates that need to be operated. Your layout plan and back story will become your personal criteria, and you can always explain away a larger box by implying that it also controls some 'off-stage' items. Alternatively, it may be justified by the removal and 'rationalization' of the local facilities, or by the provision for extra facilities that were never developed. If the interior is being modelled, you may need to incorporate a number of white 'out-of-service' levers, or vacant spaces on the frame.

Some quick research will throw up a few prototype examples and it will be immaterial where they are located; most of the original companies will have worked to similar criteria in terms of the relative size (and cost) of their installations. As a final test, try placing a paper or card mock-up in situ – if it looks wrong, it probably is.

ISSUES WITH ROOFS AND WINDOWS

There is one final point that may or may not influence the choice of material from which your kit is made. There is still, fifty years after the introduction of plastic-moulding, a problem with plastic kits. Manufacturers continue to represent the common or garden slate roof with mouldings so coarse and out of scale as to resemble, at best, clay tiles, or at worst their two-inch thick modern counterparts. It is a mystery why they cannot reproduce slate with a 'shallow-etch' effect, and why they persist with the grossly over-stated versions that usually spoil an otherwise well-crafted kit.

An example of 'scratch-building' in 12 inches-to-the-foot scale, this is at Crowcombe Heathfield on the WSR.

This ex-Bristol & Exeter Railway is at Williton on the West Somerset – another good subject for a scratch-build project.

Blue Anchor's former GWR signal box.

You might also want to consider the kit manufacturer's treatment of the main windows, which will inevitably be a dominant feature in the appearance of the box. After all, they make up almost three complete sides of the operating floor. There are a number of issues to consider: a plastic kit may be spoilt by over-thick glazing bars and frames, while a card kit may have glazing material that is too flimsy. Pre-printed glazing is often incorrect in terms of style or colour.

A careful study of the appropriate prototype images will help you to judge what is right and what is not. It is also useful to compare photographs of real-world signal boxes with the maker's images of their would-be equivalents in the featured kits. Very few will be accurate miniature versions of the prototype, but the closer they are to capturing the overall style, and the more precise and well executed their detail, the less work you will have to put in to get them visually correct.

ADDITIONS AND ALTERNATIVES

The lever frame in the signal box should have sufficient slots for every signal and point under its control. However, in both real life and on the layout, that does not necessarily apply to every signal and

point that lies within its block section. There are two notable exceptions: first, the hand-operated points within a goods yard or around the engine shed; and second, those points, and sometimes a signal or two,

Harmans Cross boasts not only a new signal box but also a completely new station.

Norden Station is at the park-and-ride end of the Swanage Railway; its busy lever frame is housed in this neat little shed.

Norden again: this new lever frame is at the commencement of the soon-to-be-operational extension to Wareham and the mainline.

which are controlled from a locally sited lever frame (although such installations will only be found at the outer limits of the block, where sight-lines are restricted and/or where there may be frequent and complicated shunting).

The first type is easy to spot on any photograph as the points will have a simple white-painted lever next to the tie-bar. These are often protected by a simple guard rail, which will also be painted white. In model form these levers are available as small white metal castings or can be quickly fabricated on the work-bench; any guard rails can also be formed from plastic rod or florist's wire. In theory they can be positioned facing the point or, more probably, parallel to the point and pulling it via a 90-degree crank. The important thing to remember is that the levers are invariably supported on extended sleepers; the space between them is hollowed out to take the mechanism. It is quite easy to make the levers yourself from small scraps of wire; they should be about 4ft (1.2m) long.

The second type is rather like a miniature, open-air signal box. As the name implies, it has a proper lever frame and can contain a mix of levers appropriate to the facilities under its control. However, it is not an autonomous unit and can only be operated with a key or token issued by the main signal box for that block. In some case, the remote frame can be activated from an unlocking lever in the box. Such a set-up would normally be found at small independent yards and sidings, where it could be worked by the train crew. Other sites are sometime found at termini where the crews could sort out their own runaround. Either way, a ground frame is not that easy to justify in model terms, but if you can find an excuse to install one, there are two versions contained in the Wills Scenics pack (around £8.00). If you find yourself with a few levers left over from one of the fairly plentiful supply in either the Springside or Ratio kits, then these can be placed within a simple scratch-built frame to give a quite satisfactory model.

The signal levers will, of course, carry the same colour codes and the frame may have bell contact with the adjacent boxes. Four or five levers would be pretty much the limit (two points, a locking lever and home/stop signals) before the frame was enclosed in a small shelter and became a signal box in its own right.

KIT OR READY-TO-SITE?

In the 1970s and 80s, there was a limited choice of signal boxes for layouts, but the options were largely adequate for most modellers' needs and this greatly simplified the decision-making process. In terms of card kits, the market was served by Bilteezi, Superquick, Metcalfe and Prototype and choices were governed by the regional setting and the amount of time the modeller wanted to

invest in the pursuit of accuracy. If you wanted to go along the plastic kit route, then it was either Ratio or the all-to-familiar Midland box from Airfix (Dapol). Ready-to-site offerings were really restricted to the very stylized Hornby(Triang) version. This was enough for most modellers to install reasonably accurate structures that were appropriate to the geographic location of the layout and to those original companies responsible the railway architecture. Anyone who needed something more precise would have to either 'kit-bash' or resort to scratch-building.

RIGHT: *Goathland box on the North York Moors railway.*

BELOW: *Goathland in miniature, courtesy of Hornby. Sadly, it is far too 'miniature', being around ten per cent under scale.*

ABOVE: *Just some of many kits currently available: the choice spans over seventy years of development, from plain printed card to the latest in downloads and laser-cut kits.*

One thing that was pretty certain was scale. With the possible exception of the Superquick kit, which was, and still is, a tad on the large side, all the other offerings were within a millimetre of the 1/76th (4mm to the foot) requirement. Despite all the many new kits, the downloads and the ready-to-site models currently available, those old favourites continue to be popular with today's enthusiasts and still grace the layouts of those who installed them several decades ago. Maybe if it ain't broke, it don't need fixing.

One of the aims of this guide is to examine the plethora of choices now available to the first-time buyer or, indeed, any modeller wishing to take a fresh look at their layout. There is now such a huge range of items out there, and so many different ways of accessing and installing them, that making the right choice is no longer straightforward. There is an enormous gulf in cost, convenience and effort between downloading a kit on to your printer and simply grabbing a ready-to-site resin box from your dealer. The second option can take just minutes, yet it will cost three or four times as much as the first, which could well take a week or so to complete.

Although the main thrust of this book is directed towards actual modelling projects, the increase in the availability and popularity of ready-to-site resin build-ings cannot be ignored. There is, however, very little that even the most committed 'customizer' can do to them. Customizing is more or less limited to a regional repaint and some extra detailing, and then only to differentiate your 'boxed box' from the countless others that walked off the shelves on the same day.

It should also be noted that the availability of these mass-market models is subject to quite acute fluctuations. At any one time, a kit may well appear in catalogues and advertisements, but be hard to find on the high street; equally, the reverse can be true, with the manufacturers' websites showing a kit out of stock while a local dealer has several on the shelf.

MAKING A COMPARISON: READY-TO-SITE VS DOWNLOAD

It should be informative to select two versions of similar, if not identical, signal boxes and take them for a 'test drive'. The ready-to-site subject is Hornby's 'Skaledale' NER box, based on the example at Goathland on the North York Moors line and currently priced at £15.50. The other box comes as a repeatable download, based on the NER one at Beamish Open Air Industrial Museum, which was

The Prototype LMS box at Stoneycombe was a stop-gap (twenty years ago!), awaiting the building of the correct GWR concrete-roofed version.

The painstaking research and superb skills of Pendon's modellers are evident in this exquisite version of Parsons Tunnel signal box. This marvellous and inspirational museum is definitely worth a visit.
ANDY YORK COURTESY PENDON MUSEUM

formerly located at Carr House East near Consett. It is currently available as a free sample download from Smart Models. (For a Smart Models assembly exercise in detail, see Chapter 5.)

With a ready-to-site model, it is always interesting to see how the contents of the polystyrene packing compare with the box artwork. My first reactions with the Hornby box were mixed. The model was neat enough and well finished, but it was a bit 'toy'-like. Perhaps this is an inevitable response from a kit- and scratch-builder when confronted with any ready-made structure, but I was also struck by its smallness. There are plenty of photographs of Goathland online, so it was reasonably easy to calculate the key dimensions. After more than half a century of 4mm modelling, my inbuilt sense of scale can tell immediately which items will fit and which will not. A quick test with a Dapol railwayman and

a ruler confirmed my worst fears: the model was woefully undersized. Several of the real-life images, which incorporated railwaymen, further proved the issue. The model seemed to be barely 75 per cent of its correct size. In scale terms, it would still be out of place on an HO layout. The actual size, by brick counting, would appear to be at least 16 x 11ft 6in, which, in our scale, equates to a model of 64 x 46mm. The model has a footprint of just 57 x 37mm. In other words, it represents a 14ft 3in by 9ft 3in box – designed for use by a very small signalman! Veteran kit-bashers and customizers can become quite adept at fettling even the least promising objects, but correcting errors of scale is impossible. Some improvement can be achieved with just a paintbrush, but the appearance of this model would have benefited from the thinning of the very chunky steps and handrails.

The resources for this model of Salisbury's Tunnel Junction box were limited to a few images in various steam albums, but the track plan and terrain made it a 'must-build'.

Not all resin offerings will display similar faults, but it does seem that many of the industrial, agricultural, domestic and railway buildings on offer in those brightly coloured 'buy-me-now' boxes will be smaller than their typical real-world prototypes. It is always wise to ask to view before purchasing, and to use a model figure for comparison. These items are not cheap – they can cost as much as £50 or more – so it is right to be cautious and discerning.

The Beamish box has no such deficiencies in terms of scale and finished appearance. The finished model comes out with 56 x 56mm footprint (14 x 14ft), which is about right, if a bit close to capacity, for the twenty-six levers contained on the frame.

NARROWING THE CHOICE

The various factors covered should prove useful to those modellers who are still making up their mind, and also to those who feel that they would like something more appropriate for an existing layout. If the layout, real or planned, is similar to the example described earlier – an isolated box with no adjacent railway buildings – the final decision will come down

If you have no room for a signal box, try a covered lever frame. This one is part (about two per cent) of the Bilteezi sheet from the 1940s.

'And now for something completely different': a beautifully restored box in the south of the Ruhr conurbation.

to a personal liking for a particular type of material. Expense may be a factor, as there is a significant difference in cost between ready-to-site models and download kits.

If the layout includes a station, as most do, the box will probably look best if it is in the same style and finish as the other buildings. This is not an absolute requirement, however, as many original structures were replaced over the years in order to meet changes in track layout and in traffic demands. It is important, however, to maintain the correct style for the chosen company and for the specific location. Plastic buildings moulded and painted to represent

brickwork can, just about, be successfully accompanied by a card kit, if it is of a predominantly wooden signal box, as long as the company style is right and the whole complex is always finished with the same paintwork.

The final factor is the one over which you will have the least control: availability. If, when you have made your ultimate and enlightened choice, you find that your local dealership is out of stock, do not be sidetracked or persuaded towards an alternative; stick to your decision and shop around. Do not waste all the effort that you have already invested. It is better to be patient than to buy in haste and repent at leisure!

CHAPTER TWO

DETAILING THE INTERIORS

BACKGROUND THOUGHTS

There is little doubt that, as any hobby develops and increases in popularity, so it inevitably spawns its own enthusiast press. To an ever-growing plethora of magazines and 'bookzines' are added forums, chat rooms, e-publishing and the wonderful world of the web. It is all good news for the modeller in search of information or inspiration. And that growth in resources always seems to be accompanied by the development of a lexicon of buzz words and 'insider speak'. This is certainly the case in the field of railway modelling. The origins of many of the more recent expressions may be lost in the archives – which editor was responsible for 'kit-bashing'? Who coined the term 'scratch-building'? Which reviewer's short-hand introduced 'r-t-r'? Which techno-wizard invented 'signal-bounce' and 'weathering' – but most of the activities described have been around in some form or other from the very beginning.

One of the most recent additions to this constantly expanding lexicon is 'vanity modelling', a term that refers to the investment in time, money and skill in creating something that will rarely, if ever, be seen. It is about a modeller going to enormous lengths to build a tank interior, down to the last bit of crewman's kit, and then cementing the hull in place. It is about a model shipwright taking care to install stokers and boilers in the bowels of a destroyer. And it is about an aircraft modeller refusing to accept that a B17 is complete without its bomb load, ammunition belts and fully detailed cockpit. In the world of railway modelling, it might mean including all the 'gubbins' that adorn the footplate of a Duchess or A4 and then adding the enginemen and hiding them all. From a personal point of view, it describes my own painstaking efforts to re-create the dusty environs of my dad's forge, from his lathe, saw-benches, pillar drills and welding gear, right down to the half-empty paint tins.

A rather quickly sketched glimpse of Corfe's operating floor designed to be viewed via a removable back wall. The figures are from the ModelU range.. The duty signalman (leaning on fresh air!) is awaiting the installation of his lever frame.

This impressive array is firmly in Southern territory at Corfe Castle on the Swanage Railway and it really does have an archetypal pot-bellied stove. The treatment of the woodwork is typical of what may be seen elsewhere, except that here the house colours are green and cream. The glass-fronted notice-board is far less common and will be an interesting item to model.

Two of the must-have details for any signal-box interior: the lever frame and the instrument shelf. For those in search of accuracy, Wills produce a plastic accessory pack and Springside offer white-metal kits for small and larger boxes. The latter is very comprehensive and includes the wire tensioners and some external items such as the point-rodding and wire guides.

If no one will see it and if only you know that it is there, why make the effort? Perhaps the answer is simply because it is a challenge to be overcome – or perhaps it is just because you want to, and if that is not 'vanity modelling', then what is? So, should you or should you not detail the interior of your signal boxes? The challenge is certainly there, and really there is no excuse not to accept it, because all the essential visual references are now easily available, from either desk research or field visits, or both.

PREPARATION

There is not a great a deal to be done here. You will need some thin card, a scrap of paper, glue, scalpel and tweezers, a measuring device (Vernier scale or dividers), watercolour paints and some house-colour enamel. (Incidentally, if you intend to do much scratch-building, a Vernier scale is a most useful acquisition. They do vary in price but, once you have one, you may well wonder how you managed before.)

The old-fashioned sink certainly looks right in Williton's compact little signal box, although the modern water-heater is probably not right for the period. A nicely polished kettle on the hob would be more appropriate. The chair looks comfortable and would be quite easy to model.

You will need a selection of images, relevant to the chosen box and its intended role and preferably in colour. (Be aware that coloured photographs from the steam era are virtually non-existent and even mono versions are scarce.) Last but not least, you need to decide whether the white-metal Springside kit(s) or the Wills plastic version, or indeed some other alternative, is best suited to the key features in this task.

The task will demand a degree of ingenuity and some physical dexterity, as it involves convincingly fixing many small items into a very confined space. As the intention is to fit out the inside of a kit-built box, it is obvious that there will be no exact prototype images to follow. However, contemporary photographs will show a broad selection of all the 'fixtures and fittings' that could find a place on the operating floor of your box. First, you need to decide which of the kit components you can justify and that means taking a critical look at what role the box has in your particular story. To give some simple examples: the very attractive level-crossing capstan is obviously required only if there is a crossing for it to operate; if the box is on the mainline, then the token apparatus is not needed; you can take a gamble with the number of levers that you want to include,

based on the size of the box and its location; similarly, you may wish to shorten the instrument shelf or remove some of its features. The second job is to check which of the possible additional features have been supplied with the kit (and are of use) and which other essential items are missing and will therefore need to be fabricated.

VIEWING AND ACCESSIBILITY

Once you have a good idea of what you want to include, you need to consider how to fit everything (correctly) into the available space and whether you wish to make it accessible for close-up inspection. The first should be a 'constant'. Whether the interior is to be merely glimpsed through the windows, or whether some part of the box will be removable, there is still a place for everything and everything must be in its place. Even 'vanity modelling' should not allow for obvious mistakes or a slap-dash approach.

The second decision, regarding accessibility, will be governed by two further key factors. The first of these, and it too might be termed a 'constant', is the technical feasibility of the idea, given the obvious constraints of the design of the kit or your own abilities as a scratch-builder. The second factor involves

The interior of Williton signal box: simple and efficient, but still 'home'. Note the use of BR(w) 'chocolate' on the panelling and cupboards, the crowded desk with its train-register and the essential stool. Some of the equipment is current, but the furled flags are ever present. The eagle eyed observer may have spotted the single-line token hanging from the instrument shelf.

The familiar capstan and brown levers control Blue Anchor's level-crossing. Those heavy gates take some shifting, especially when the high winds sweep in off the Bristol Channel.

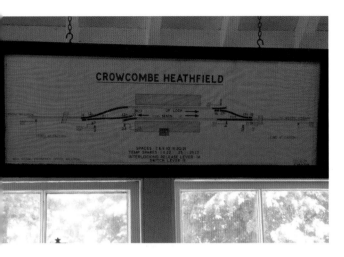

The signal-box diagram is essential if you are detailing the interior; but if you only want the partial glimpse through the window, then any small scrap of card or plastic will suffice.

East Ilsley signal box in a scratch-built rendition of the typical GWR wartime 'ARP' style. The interior has been assembled with floor and the back wall as a one-piece push-in sub-assembly.

choosing the preferred method of achieving that sought-after accessibility. There are five possible options:

Removable roof: this is probably the most obvious and widely used method. It can be applied to most kits, card, plastic or download, and is certainly well within the capabilities of the average scratch-

builder. Its downsides (and these are not critical) are that it only gives a bird's-eye view of the carefully modelled interior and it also poses the question of how to install the hanging features, such as the instrument shelf and diagram.

Removable wall: this also has its limitations but, if the technical issues are properly resolved, it does give a better eye-level or visitor's view of the operating floor. It is important to ensure that the three-sided box is square and robust, and that the back wall is a snug fit but still easy to remove.

Removable floor: this is an extra that can be used in conjunction with the previous version. The box is assembled with the operating floor in place, but acting as a simple shelf on which to slide a detailed floor made up on thin card or plastic sheet. With the back wall removed, the entire floor can be slid out and admired from every angle.

Removable wall/floor: this effectively combines both the above. In this version the floor is permanently fixed to the back wall and the whole sub-assembly is pulled out for viewing.

Removable top section: this may seem to be a rather drastic solution but, in reality, it is only an extension of the removable roof idea – figuratively and literally! The concept is simple enough: the lower floor is assembled in the usual way, with the fully detailed operating floor permanently installed as its 'lid'. The roof is also completed normally, but then the four glazed and detailed upper walls are attached to it rather than the other way around. This whole sub-assembly then sits squarely on top of the lower section but remains easy to lift off for viewing. While this may prove a difficult option for a kit-builder, it should be within the scope of a scratch-builder. The questions of fit, bracing and 'securing' are down to the individual, but the idea should have particular appeal to anyone modelling a box with a brickwork base and wooden upper floor.

The following chapters will include some of these five variations as applied to suitable kit and scratch-build projects.

Finally, there are two ways of completing an eventual permanent installation; the most obvious is to

The interior of the small scratch-built version of Dainton signal box on the 'Wessex Lines' layout. All the items were simply knocked together from scraps found in the bits box (but the token apparatus still needs painting correctly!).

simply work inside the model and juggle the various items to get the best fit before gluing them down. The alternative, and on balance the better, method is to create a 'drop-in' or 'slide-in' interior on the work-bench. This gives you far more control, enables a higher standard of modelling and requires considerably less dexterity. Since the first method is quite easy to understand, even if it can be tricky to execute, the second method will be covered in more detail here. (Inevitably, some of this advice will be encountered again when describing the assembly or construction of the respective signal boxes.)

INTERIOR DETAILING: METCALFE PLUS SPRINGSIDE

This 'box-within-a-box' approach is applicable to any interior-detailing project and not just to signal boxes. Like so much of modelling, it is more complicated and time-consuming to explain than it is to actually do! It starts with getting some accurate measurements to create templates for the floor and all four walls. The measurements for the walls must of course include the apertures for the existing windows and

provision for the necessary doors and stove area. The measurements are drawn on copy paper and cut out, initially in a trial version. Once they have been checked, and amended if necessary, they can be transferred to the actual work-piece, using suitably thin card. The example used for the exercise was the Metcalfe kit.

The basic template can now be treated almost like a mini 3D stage set. Begin by gently scribing the four lines where the walls meet the floor in order to bend them upright to help you design and fit the various items. Some adjustments as you go along are almost inevitable when attempting a 'retro-fit' into an existing structure. It is very much about getting things broadly right to begin with, and then repeatedly offering up and refining until an acceptable stage is reached.

THE OPERATING FLOOR

The operating floor of a signal box was usually covered with brown linoleum or left as highly polished floorboards. These can be simply painted on with satin brown enamel (or similar). Cut the lever frame to the size appropriate for the planned

Blue Anchor's larger box clearly anticipates more regular visitors. The question about the provision of chairs is a controversial one. There are those who insist that nothing more comfortable than a basic chair was ever allowed, while others favour the domestic fireside chair – at the very least. Presumably, it had something to do with the amount of traffic being dealt with, the number of staff on duty and, ultimately, the attitude of the S & T Inspector.

Chocolate and cream again together with yet another type of heating installation. Woe betide the unwary visitor who soiled that polished lino.

Not all signal boxes had the later free-standing round stove. The Bristol & Exeter men could warm their midday snack in the neat little oven.

number of levers and glue it in place. It should be centred on the middle of the floor and located two or three feet (8 to 12mm) in from the front. Paint it with 'gunmetal', metallic or satin black. One interesting feature is a plain wooden plank on the floor side of the frame: this would prevent the signalman doing himself a mischief by slipping on his own highly polished lino! Do not install the levers yet, but do fix the crossing capstan at the appropriate end of the frame if that applies on your version.

The other item that must have a fixed position is the obligatory source of warmth. It would appear that the traditional Victorian 'pot-bellied' was by no means universal. Many boxes were graced by what was, to all intents and purposes, a miniature kitchen range. Of course, it is difficult to determine which of these two was fitted in any particular box, but if there is a proper brick or stone-built chimney, it seems probable that the box had a range. If, however, the chimney is the familiar metal flue, it is probably connected to

a stove. Nothing is absolute, however, and you could not be faulted for modelling a stove whose flue then disappears into an original chimney. As long as you position it directly below the chimney, all will be well. One minor point is that the stove or range usually stood on a solid metal tray, presumably to prevent an over-heated device burning its way through the floorboards and descending into the locking room! If you have a stove in your kit, that is obviously the one to use. If not, the accompanying illustrations may inspire some cheap and cheerful fabrications.

WALLS AND FITTINGS

In most railway interiors – and, indeed, in the majority of public buildings of the same period – the walls featured a lower half clad in vertical panelling, usually painted in the house colour, and upper sections of whitewashed plaster, or white-painted planking in a wooden box. Some heritage railways use cream rather than white so there may be precedence for this. Both are easy to reproduce with enamels and watercolours.

At this point, it is a good idea to bend the walls upright and gauge how much (or how little!) space will be left for all the other fixtures and fittings. It is surprising how much may be squeezed into these relatively small structures; since this is 'vanity modelling', and therefore without any timetable or strategic objective, I decided to see just what I could include without making the whole thing too fanciful. For the purposes of this exercise, some of the items from the larger detailing kit by Springside were used, along with a few scratch-built pieces of furniture or decoration to complete the scene. The Springside kit is certainly comprehensive, with almost enough equipment to complete two boxes of this size.

THE LEVER FRAME AND 'STAGE SET'

This box was envisaged as being located somewhere along a twin-track secondary mainline, controlling a level-crossing. The arrangement of levers in this box would be unlikely to satisfy the signalling purist, but they do run fairly logically from left (up) to right (down) – distant, outer-home, home, points/interlocking levers, up-starter, home, outer-home, distant and then the two brown levers to release the gates – with the gate capstan to the right of the frame. Those signals furthest from the box have the wire-adjusters fitted on the far side. The one basic

'Between trains' at Crowcombe: the paperwork on the desk is typical but those GWR logos are a personal touch.

Interiors may have differed in their detail but the basics were always the same. In Corfe Castle on the Swanage Railway (the plentiful green paintwork is a bit of a giveaway), the white levers are 'not in use' and the token exchange mechanism sits on the cupboards at the far end.

rule is that lever-release must always be nearest the window and facing away from the signalman.

It is a matter of choice whether to paint the levers before or after gluing them to the frame. A fine brush is of course essential, as is the knowledge of the correct colours to use. The most obvious ones are as follows: home/stop, red; distant, yellow; points, black; inter-locking, blue; level-crossing locks, brown; and out-of-use/spare, white. The base of the levers and the back should be metallic and match the frame. The top should be as shiny as possible; a good-quality silver enamel would do, but chrome would be even better.

Using the dummy shelf supports to suspend the instrument shelf from a pair of cross-members gave me the opportunity to fabricate the essential signal-box diagram (the only thing missing from the kit). This was fixed between the supports. Despite it not being single-track, I installed the simpler of the two token machines, to represent the type for issuing releases during occupancies by the local gangers.

Apart from the various traffic notices, some pictures, a newspaper, a facsimile 'Shops, Offices and Factories Act' notice and a vase of flowers, nothing extra was needed for the 'stage set'. I did go for the crowded-box option and added a number of role-playing figures. The signalman is pulling off one of the points, his relief is signing on, a fireman has just entered under 'Rule 55' and the bowler-hatted Inspector is showing family visitors around his domain. It makes an attractive, albeit unlikely, scene. It is the ultimate in vanity modelling!

INTERIOR DETAILING: AIRFIX/DAPOL BOX

There are a number of potential difficulties with this sort of project. The usual method for detailing any interior is either to work on everything in situ, or to work up a false floor and drop it into place, then install the detachable or fixed roof. When it comes to this kit, the false-floor option is probably the better option, together with a detachable roof. However, the roof is not as easy as it might be, having only small locating ribs with which to get its position correct.

TOP AND ABOVE: *The finished interior of the Metcalfe box, showing some of the visitors that might have been encountered, albeit rarely all at once. The duty signalman is working the frame, his relief is signing on, an Inspector is entertaining a small family and a fireman has wandered in to report under Rule 55.*

ABOVE LEFT AND RIGHT: *The essential signal-box diagram can either be supported as part of the instrument-shelf assembly or suspended from the roof trusses. Choose whichever fixing is easiest, as long as it is positioned above the instrument shelf. It will only ever be just glimpsed through the windows in normal operations.*

ABOVE LEFT AND RIGHT: *The centre portion of the detailing destined for the Airfix/Dapol box. It is much easier to compose these little stage sets on the work-bench rather than trying to fix them through the roof. The basic furniture and wall-fixings were installed during assembly.*

Even then, when securing it, it is best to invert the box and work from within the void created by the missing floor. That is the issue: fit the floor and roof is difficult to secure; fit the roof and it is impossible to insert the detailed floor. Any slight warping to the roof will further compound the problem.

The solution is to split the detailing into several parts. First, measure, make and test-fit the false floor so it can be inserted from underneath and can eventually be fixed to the narrow strips of floor already provided. Paint it, and the strips, and then set it aside. Second, make and install all the features that can be fixed to the walls and that can be stood on those narrow strips. Third, make all the other desired bits and pieces that will be located in the central area of the false floor. Have a 'dry run' with the floor held in place and mark or memorize the optimum position of each item. Remove the floor and glue them down, double-checking that they will all clear the strips and any overhanging items. Set this sub-assembly to one side.

Invert the box and carefully glue the roof into its correct position, then, with fingers firmly crossed, run a seam of cement round the outside of the floor and press it firmly home against the underside of the strips.

Of course, ideally you would use the normal method and the detachable roof, but, even if your own particular roof moulding is 100 per cent true and warp-free, the final fit is still likely to be poor and precarious. It is inevitable that there will be slight differences in all kits, so every modeller will have to decide which route is the more practical and possible.

For the record, this detailing exercise took well over twenty hours, or five times as long as the kit itself. The lever frame and instrument shelf were leftovers from the Springside pack and all the other items were knocked up from oddments of card and pieces from the 'bits box'. All that effort is scarcely visible with the roof in place, so it is certainly a fine example of 'vanity modelling'.

MAKING THE BOX MOVABLE

The removable roof is not the only way of providing access to the interior of a signal box. Sometimes you will need to be a bit more adventurous if you want to create a setting that is both accurate and full of atmosphere. Building the operating floor 'off-stage' allows you to retain full control of every detail, and work on it from every angle, but it can be tricky inserting the finished item into the box. On an exhibition layout particularly, the floor will need to be secured against movement, and, in order to make the handiwork visible to visitors and colleagues, the box, as well as all or part of the roof, will need to be movable.

The many items for inclusion within the Wills kit are being fixed to the operating floor, which is a 'slide-in' assembly, resting on a permanently cemented false floor. The back wall has some minimal detailing and can be glued in place or left detachable so the interior can be easily withdrawn and admired.

In the case of the war-time box for East Ilsley, this problem was further aggravated by the presence of the flat concrete roof that is so much a feature of the design. Finding a solution involved much head-scratching as well as scratch-building. The eventual answer was to build the floor off-stage and then fix it to an equally detailed back wall. This sub-assembly could then be a simple push-fit insert into the rest of the box, which, in turn, could sit in a shallow recess in the ballast. It is now easy to remove the whole box for transits, and both the box and the wall for any discussions with visitors.

The same basic approach is used on the Wills box, but with one significant difference: the detailed floor remains 'loose' and sits on the sturdy original floor, which is needed to maintain the structural integrity of the box as a whole. The rear wall, with its own detail, is then clipped between the gable ends. The interior work may be shown off by unclipping the rear wall and sliding the floor out. This method also enables eye-level viewing, which is not possible with the removable roof. The idea may not work for every kit, with the various different assembly processes, but its advantages make it worth considering. It is certainly an option on all scratch-builds, where the modeller has total control over their own 'kit design' and construction process.

The idea for the removable floor was driven by the notion of creating a multi-user sub-assembly. The plan was to use it again in other boxes, to save the time, effort and cost of building a new floor for each one. Do not be too surprised, therefore, if some of the interiors look rather familiar….

'HUMINIATURES'

When creating interiors and working on detailing in general, you should also consider the 'huminiatures' that might be included. The most important of these, and probably the only one that is really necessary, is the signalman himself, or the 'Bobby', as they were still being called more than a century after the last one waved his red flag! The choice of 4mm (1/76th) figures is far from extensive, so it is usually a case of finding a general-purpose railwayman in a pose that might be suitable for his new role.

First, you will need to consider all the personnel required, and the activities that might be going on in the box at any given time. For the sake of the exercise, let us look at a box of fourteen to twenty levers, with an operating floor of somewhere between 18ft and 25ft in length by 10ft and 15ft wide. Such a box would probably be open during daylight hours only and would be worked by two shifts. Very few boxes of this size would be open for twenty-four hours a day and therefore require the third shift. However, nothing is absolute; the important thing is to work with your own box and with anything else that is relevant to your overall 'back story':

- **Signalman:** pulling a lever, turning the level-crossing wheel, speaking on the phone, completing the train register, using the telegraph, making a 'cuppa', tending the stove, sitting with the paper, nursing the station cat, taking a breather on the veranda, signing off, opening in the window, displaying a flag from the window, cleaning the window, or just watching the world go by. (The first may seem the most likely pose, and it is certainly the most commonly modelled, yet it is not that frequent an activity and has also become almost as much of a cliché as the ever-shovelling fireman!)
- **Relief signalman:** arriving with his bike, entering or leaving on the veranda, signing on, chatting to his colleague, or helping out on any of the jobs in the first list.
- **Trainee:** just watching or chatting with his senior colleague(s), or completing the register. (This need not be a younger figure, as many senior ex-footplate men transferred to S & T as steam jobs declined.)
- **Inspector:** perhaps escorting the trainee, sitting observing the signalman or chatting with him.
- **Station Master:** if the box is part of the station complex, it will almost certainly receive at least one visit every day from the Station Master. He might also choose to accompany the inspector.
- **Fireman (visiting):** arriving or signing-in under Rule 55.

The signalman in action in Blue Anchor box – a nice pose to try to capture if your detailing kit includes the capstan wheel. If it does not, you may find a suitable substitute among the model-boat accessories.

A perfect little scene to re-create, as the porter drops in for a chat between trains at Crowcombe on the WSR. The very prominent token apparatus on its chocolate and cream cabinets is also quite visible from outside the box.

- **Ganger (visiting):** notifying the box that the track gang are arriving or leaving the section.
- **Civilians:** a local schoolboy 'spotter', perhaps a friendly photographer, or maybe even a small family who are no doubt related to the Inspector or Station Master!
- **Off-duty railwayman:** many signal boxes boasted a small vegetable plot close by, and off-duty figures could almost always be seen tending the crop or discussing their gardening efforts with the signalman. Where the box is located on or at the end of a platform, such visits would be more frequent.

There are at least nine different individuals that could be included, and dozens of reasons for them to be in the box. Of course, not all of them would be there at the same time, but it does mean that the scene can feature much more than one lone signalman grappling with a stubborn lever.

Once you have decided that you are going to indulge yourself and design a viewable interior, you have to find the most suitable figures to fulfil the various roles, not forgetting that British Railways in the 1950s employed a significant number of women in its signal boxes. For a number of years, the choice has been limited to Dapol (plastic), Monty's Models (white-metal), or possibly Langley. For those who could accept differences in scale, Preisers offered the most exquisitely executed figures, which simply oozed character, and it was also worth checking old military figures for any possibles. In very recent times, however, a completely new range of figures has become available from ModelU Finescale Figures, using the very latest in 3D printing technology. Already, there are over fifty 4mm models on offer, reproduced as fully detailed plastic figures from 2D images, with more subjects in the pipeline, including some much-needed fixtures and fittings. These exquisite little huminiatures have a practical

Recent developments in 3D printing are being put to good use by ModelU. Their increasing range of figures and accessories in the three main scales make a welcome, and long overdue, addition to the modeller's armoury. The poses and 'sculpting' are excellent.

Some signalmen were issued with a sleeved waistcoat, partly as protection, partly for warmth, and partly to enable easier movement. It was the usual black serge and the added sleeves appear to have been in waxed cotton. The figure on the left has the traditional waistcoat, worn over a blue shirt, while the other wears the sleeved version.

snap-off base and like-life poses, and are competitively priced.

There were distinct similarities between the uniforms worn by service personnel and those issued to railway employees, so it is wise to study contemporary images of signal-box interiors, and pay particular attention to the dress code of the staff. Simply search on 'BR uniforms 1950s'. Some signalmen were issued with sleeved waistcoats, which presumably provided more warmth and protection than the serge jacket, without its restrictions. These are not the easiest items to paint on a figure less than an inch tall!

EXTERNAL DETAILING AND STRUCTURAL DETAILS

There is plenty of opportunity for details outside the box as well as inside. The duty signalman's mode of transport is a must; in the 1950s, this might well have been a motorcycle, perhaps covered with a bit of tarpaulin, an old sack or a discarded raincoat. In these later years, the signalman's wage packet might even have stretched to a second-hand car, although he would not necessarily have been able to park right next to the box! The ubiquitous red fire buckets are essential and a primitive coal bunker or heap of coal would also be a likely feature. If the gangers were working locally, their bikes could well have been left there – ladies' bikes would definitely be among that number, as they were much favoured by those more elderly workers.

The whimsical touch of roses round the door would certainly grab attention and is not without precedence, but it is probably best avoided outside of the branch-line or rural box. That said, depending on the size, shape and suitability of the area around the box, a small vegetable plot might certainly be in order.

A smaller box with a modelled interior that still lacks the important exterior items that could contribute so much to its character and role on the layout. There is a signalman stepping out for a breather, or perhaps coming off shift, but a coal heap, fire buckets, bicycles and other items would all give it more of a lived-in look.

Structural details will be mentioned later in relation to customizing or improving the signal box itself, but at this stage a study of archive images will yield plenty of ideas: finials, barge-boards, drainpipes and guttering, telephone dolls, safety rails, fire buckets, lighting (especially on platform-mounted boxes), a wooden walkway/protection over the emerging point-rodding and signal wires will all add character and purpose to the box.

CHAPTER THREE

ASSEMBLING AND IMPROVING CARD KITS

A BRIEF OVERVIEW

With the wide range of signal-box kits available and the large number of ready-to-site buildings, the would-be S & T engineer is certainly spoilt for choice. So where do you start?

Every modeller will have their own particular requirements that will influence their decision. Somewhere on the list of criteria will be the need to build a box that is correct for their company/ BR region and appropriate to their chosen locality. They will also want it to match any other existing or planned station buildings – indeed, this may well prove to be the key factor. Some other considerations are the nature of the kit (card, plastic, download, laser-cut or etch), the cost, the ease of construction, the relative size and the time and skills it will demand to get the optimum result. The order of priority on the list will vary with each modeller.

Rather than taking up the challenge of assembling each and every kit that is currently available, I have used a more logical approach and created a shortlist of the most popular models, covering the three most common mediums, as well as a broad range of sizes and prices. Each kit has been built according to the instructions, and then the options for customization have been explored, so that they may be adapted to different roles or locations. Any simple improvements that may be incorporated into the initial build (either to aid construction or to enhance the finished product) will also be highlighted.

The advice will begin with some of the card kits, moving on to the plastic versions before finishing with some of the more recent downloads and laser-cut options. It will not cover the half-dozen or so brass etches, as this would be advancing from the hobby table to the workshop. Where they are relevant (or no longer easily available), some additional examples from the boxes already located on Wessex Lines will be added.

BILTEEZI

Bilteezi has been in existence for nearly seventy years. Like all the models in this quite extensive range, this one was designed and drawn by C. Vacey-Ash in 1947/48, around the time of the end of the Big Four and the birth of the nationalized British Railways. It was also the era when the country was in the grip of the post-war Austerity Period and when the notion of scenic modelling was still in its infancy. With both raw materials and money in short supply, the simplicity of the Bilteezi concept was a masterful solution. All the kits, from the signal box to the warehouse or Tudor mansion, consist of simple single card sheets of a constant size and price. What they may lack in terms of substance and relief detail, they make up for with their character and artwork, superb print quality and intriguing design. While they may not match up to the more recent Metcalfe kits, they do compare quite favourably against the latest downloads, with whom they share the principle of flat artwork on a shell of thicker reinforcing card. They are also commendably colour-fast – the scores of examples on my 'Wessex Lines' have graced its countryside for over thirty years with no signs of deterioration, despite the often hostile environment of a loft layout.

Bilteezi kits can still be found in many model shops and on the stalls of those dealers who mainly concentrate on exhibitions or toy fairs. This sample was supplied by Freestone Models, specialists in card kits, via their mail-order service. Priced at

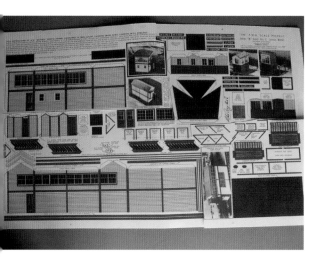

The Bilteezi kit comes as one sheet of artwork, which also includes the instructions and various tips. It is advisable to cut it into a number of segments to make it easier to handle.

To avoid seeing a maze of white edges on a completed card kit, where possible you should paint before fixing. It is a good idea to paint from the back of the piece to avoid over-running on to the actual artwork.

The corner overlays can be applied only when the main shell of the building is finished. They are quite tricky to get right as you rarely have more than a couple of millimetres either side of the fold. Try scoring them a bit deeper and bending them double between thumb and finger before fixing. Use the flat of your scalpel blade to press and smooth the overlay.

The larger of the two Bilteezi signal boxes nearing completion, with only the veranda and external stairs to be tackled.

Most components rely on the score-and-bend approach, which is best done when the work-piece is whole. Always aim for a 100 per cent accurate score-line – a steel straight-edge is essential.

The finished 'box' ready for the wraparound artwork. It is best to detail the artwork as fully as you can before fixing it to the carcass.

Cutting foamboard is easy: use a sharp blade, straight-edge and keep the scalpel vertical. One cut, or two at most, should be all that is needed. These are the four sides and false floors that will make up into the 'box'. Any type of PVA adhesive will be suitable, but remember to keep checking that everything is properly square and vertical while the glue is setting.

between £2.00 and £3.00, the sheet includes two signal boxes, two 'sheds' for ground frames and numerous detailing items.

Assembly is quite straightforward, but it is sensible to read through the instructions before starting. It does rely on some careful cutting out using a sharp scalpel or suitable craft knife; this kit used no fewer than six blades. A decent-quality PVA adhesive, applied with a dispenser, brush or palette knife, is the only glue you should need, although it is worth keeping a tube of clear glue at hand. You will need mounting board or foamboard for added strength and durability (keep small off-cuts of board from other jobs for this purpose), and this can be fixed with the PVA or even a glue-stick. The name 'Bilteezi' says it all and even an absolute beginner should encounter few difficulties; at the same time, the experienced modeller should enjoy the challenge of the extra effort needed to help realize the full potential of the kits.

The larger box was modelled exactly in accordance with the instructions, but then a few cosmetic retro-improvements were carried out. The smaller box, on the other hand, was enhanced as part of the normal assembly process. In order to demonstrate alternative methods, the larger version was built around a complete foamboard box, while the smaller one used mounting board in the traditional way.

ASSEMBLING THE LARGER BILTEEZI BOX

There is not a great deal to be said about this part of the project, but the key point to remember from the outset is that you are dealing with relatively flimsy card; it will certainly seem that way if you are accustomed to Superquick and Metcalfe kits. To some extent, you are almost entering the world of scratch-building where the strength and finish of your structures depends entirely upon the accuracy of your own measurements.

The technique of building an internal box and viewing the artwork as a continuous wrapper around all four sides is not revolutionary; it is no more than a variation of the more common method of folding the reinforced sides into the eventual box. The secret is to ensure that each side exactly matches its particular wall and that all the sides meet at a perfect right-angle inside the corners of the outer artwork. The one main advantage is, at

Despite two or three hours of fiddling, folding, re-folding, re-scoring and re-gluing, the end was a disaster. It was time to have a re-think and revert to the traditional method of building steps and staircases (components on the right).

The veranda and stairs are often tricky to get right, and it is almost impossible to disguise any shortcomings.

Patience and persistence do pay off and this time the stairs, veranda and safety rails have been satisfactorily assembled. The many windows could then be enhanced using either a gloss gel pen or gloss varnish; the improvement is only marginal but it is still worth the effort.

Two location shots of the larger Bilteezi signal box, the first at Knighton Yard and the second on the coast at Torpoint. It makes a neat, tidy and robust structure.

least in my experience, that it makes it easier to install the false floor and ceiling. The use of foamboard on this method is to demonstrate how easy it is to work and how its thickness (5mm plus) is better suited to box construction than the much thinner mounting board.

The assembly is straightforward, with the exception of the veranda, rails and stairs.

ASSEMBLING THE SMALLER BILTEEZI BOX

The initial stages of any 'customizing' project involve first deciding the end result you want to achieve, and then to figure out how best to achieve it. Studying the artwork of this box resulted in three snap decisions: the windows would be cut out and replaced, the veranda and steps would also go; and, with the larger expanse of planned glazing, some interior detailing would become essential. The roof assembly rather ruled it out as a potentially movable feature so, for access and viewing, it would have to be the detach-

The smaller of the two boxes was assembled in the traditional way, with mounting board used to reinforce the walls and to provide the necessary false floors. Note that the printed windows have been removed and replaced with the correct glazed versions.

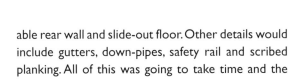

ABOVE: *The new glazing is the typical GWR 'three-over-two' five-pane style. The sheets are available from several sources; these are from Prototype, supplied by Freestone Models. They are not an exact fit so they have been cut and fixed as if they were partly opened.*

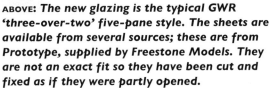

ABOVE RIGHT AND RIGHT: *There is very little room for interior detailing in such a small box, but it was possible to knock up and paint something quick and cheap from scrap card. This was then slipped in on top of the false floor and the back wall glued in place.*

able rear wall and slide-out floor. Other details would include gutters, down-pipes, safety rail and scribed planking. All of this was going to take time and the usual amount of trial and error.

My first impression that both these boxes were largely GWR in origin proved well founded, as the only glazing that would fit the eventual cut-outs was Prototypes sheet for their Western signal box. It was correct for the height of the windows but wrong in respect of their spacing. The answer was to model one set of sliding panes in the 'open' position in order to disguise the error.

From this point, the build was quite straightforward and the finished box turned out to be more or less as intended. It would not look at all out of place on any wayside station or branch-line terminus.

It is a tribute to the soundness of Bilteezi's original design that, even after sixty years, albeit with a bit of extra TLC, these signal boxes can still hold their own among today's models.

LEFT: *There is not a lot that can be done retrospectively to any Bilteezi kit, with the possible exceptions of gutters, down-pipes and chimneys. The rather large name-board is quite impressive and the partly open window reveals some of the detail and gives a lived-in look.*

BELOW: *The completed small signal box, enhanced during its assembly, makes a handsome little model as it does its duty at Winterbourne.*

GROUND-FRAME HUTS

The Bilteezi sheet also includes two 'mini kits' of typical ground-frame shelters. The first, although it is not identified as such, appears to be the small pitched-roof version found in many former GWR locations. The second is actually described as 'Midland/LMS' in origin with larger windows and a simple arc roof. Having just assembled the sets of lever frames (see Chapter 4), it seemed a worthwhile diversion to see if this little building would actually serve its intended purpose. A quick offer-up showed it that it might and that, with a bit of extra effort, it could make quite a neat little feature.

That was Sunday evening gone by the wayside! It quickly became clear that building the hut as per the instructions would be pretty pointless, as the lever frame would then be invisible. The answer

In addition to the two signal boxes, the Biteezi kit also provides for two small lever-frame huts – this is the Midland version. They are a bit of fiddle to get right!

CLOCKWISE, FROM TOP LEFT: *For comparison purposes, the Watlingford branch terminus on 'Wessex Lines', with its usual small Prototype box replaced first by the Bilteezi lever frame and then by the smaller of their two signal boxes.*

was to model it with the door fully opened and the printed windows replaced by transparent ones. If that was not enough to contemplate on a structure measuring less than four square centimetres, the plan was also to try to preserve the printed glazing bars and scribe the individual planks. As it turned out, even with a new blade in the scalpel the bars were just too fine to remain intact. In addition, that new blade made it hard to differentiate between scribed planks and the score-and-bend corners. In the end it came down to plastiglaze and white gel pen for the windows and some 'fudging' on the corners. It was six hours of hard labour, but at least the result was a passable little addition. It is worth a go, but it would be wise not to attempt scribing the planks and to go straight for the fully cut-out windows.

SUPERQUICK

Superquick has also been around for several decades and has remained largely unaltered in that time. Like all the first-generation of Superquick kits, this one is best described as 'generic' rather than an attempt to reproduce any particular prototype. Indeed, there is nothing in any of the albums or on any of the websites that looks remotely like it. However, it may be feasible to carry out some simple retrospective customizing in an effort to achieve something different and more realistic.

The artwork is in the same style as Superquick's other railway buildings and represents a medium-sized wood-framed mainline box. It has a frontage of 104mm (26ft), which suggests at least twenty levers – excessive even for a larger branch-line terminus. The bonus offerings in the kit, including a Coal Order Office and lineside huts, go some way to mitigating its £7.50 price tag, which is a bit on the high side for a kit that does not compare too well with its slightly more expensive competitor from Metcalfe.

BASIC PREPARATIONS

As always, it is advisable to read through the instructions before beginning the assembly process. Indeed, if this is your first kit-build exercise, it might be wise

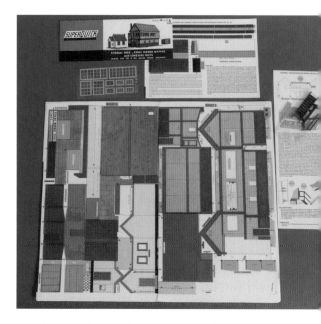

The Superquick pack is a familiar sight in most if not all hobby and model shops. The signal box is another long-term survivor and was among their initial series of launches.

Some of these earlier kits do need the intervention of a scalpel or craft knife to separate the components. Just pushing them out will risk damaging the laminated card.

to put in a bit of practice and assemble the additional buildings first. The box will be assembled according to the designer's instructions, and then you can see what might be done to improve its 'prototypicality'.

The instructions are perfectly adequate and the kit should be well within the capabilities of any first-time builder. Little is needed in the way of preparation except to start with a new blade and ensure that the components are cleanly cut from the frets. They are supposed to be pop-outs, but they are sometimes a tad reluctant to separate themselves from the sheets. It is also advisable to have bracing pieces to hand for the corners; these can be triangular off-cuts from scrap on the sheets or some quarter-inch square balsa wood. A decent-quality PVA – not too little but not too much – is the ideal adhesive. The instructions recommend secure the glazing with Sellotape, but this is not ideal. The windows are already a weak point, being on a thin sheet and finished with yellow glazing bars, and Sellotape does dry out and become brittle over time. This problem is not helped when it is used on absorbent card surfaces, so it is better to make careful use of any universal clear glue such as UHU.

Always pay particular attention to the window areas. It may be necessary to push the blade into the corners to ensure a nice clean edge.

MAKING IMPROVEMENTS

In terms of the basic assembly, there was some difficulty with the back wall, but there are certain revisions that may be made. None is particularly time-consuming and they will all help to produce a robust and acceptable end product for any layout that is not striving for prototypical accuracy. Initial improvements could include scoring all the planks and the tile courses; reducing the size of the roof; making the roof detachable and re-planning the barge-boards and guttering.

The following suggestions show what might be done to an already completed box. It may be one on your own layout to which you want to give a quick face-lift, or it may be an item acquired second-hand from a toy fair. However, many of the jobs will be even easier if they are done on a new kit as part of the assembly process. These are by no means the only options, and a browse through all the resources may well throw up other possibilities more to your liking

It is far from essential to scribe the individual planks, but it is effective on those sections that will face the viewer.

and more in keeping with the buildings already on your layout. Whichever option appeals to you, always keep an eye on the likely investment of time and cost. There is little point in spending too much on what will still be compromise version, especially if a more accurate kit is already available.

It is hard to find a prototype to use as a guide. Most ex-GWR and LSWR boxes are way out; the former LNER versions seem possible, as do some Midland boxes, as long as you ignore their predominantly hipped-roof styling. In the end, a Saxby & Farmer version frequently found on the SECR/SR lines in the south-east was chosen. This entailed little more than an extensive repaint and some additional detailing. Any other changes are really just cosmetic, to enhance the difference.

Before you get too Involved In the proposed changes, there is one little trick that you may find useful. Simply cut out those parts of the kit on which you intend to work – usually the two main walls and the gable ends – and run off two or three mono copies. You can then scribble all over them, cut them up further or generally test your ideas in any way you choose, without risking the initial integrity of the kit. This photocopying is just about possible even with a fully assembled model, although you will probably have to forego the gable end with steps and outside toilet.

Before getting too carried away with this transformation exercise, it is as well to highlight three design shortcomings:

1) The veranda/walkway across the front of the box has no guard rails, which, even before the advent of Health & Safety legislation, would have been unacceptable. However, this can be rectified (see the finished product).

2) Another H & S issue: the access stairs protrude some 4 feet beyond the front of the box, which means the poor old signalman will be run down by passing freight long before he has the chance to fall in its path from his unguarded veranda! Once the box is built, there is not much that can be done to remedy this. However, with little ingenuity during the initial build, or if it is not too firmly fixed, it should be possible (just) to rotate the stairs 90

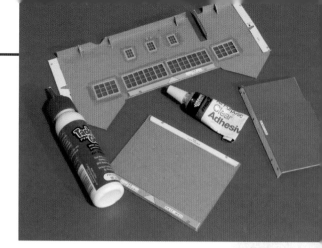

The window sheet provided with the kit suffers from the usual Superquick shortcoming of yellow frames and glazing bars. This can be replaced with something more appropriate or carefully 'overpainted' using a mapping pen or white ballpoint. Always use a clear or universal glue to fix them in place; Deluxe Glue 'n' Glaze gives good results. Take care not to apply too much adhesive, keep it clear of the window panes and beware of sticky fingers.

The kit makes up into quite a large structure, especially when compared to other versions. It is worth adding extra bracing at the corners to prevent distortion, checking each stage with your square.

degrees to the left and mount the handrail on their right.

3) Any door from the lobby on to the operating floor is going to open directly against the stove, which is obviously right in that corner. It should have been at the opposite end (see the Williton box in Chapter 1). The only solution would be to

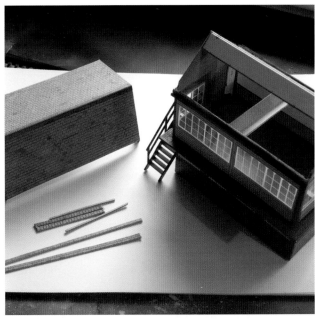

The entrance lobby and veranda are done as a sub-assembly. They need to be firmly and accurately fixed to the main building; use firm hand pressure to squeeze them together while the glue sets.

With the building completed, bar any interior details and securing the roof, it is a useful exercise to offer it (and indeed any similar structure) up on the layout. Hopefully there will be no unpleasant surprises!

Once you have confirmed that it fits, the final details such as the safety rails and moderate weathering can be completed.

The box complete and ready for permanent installation. It has turned out to look typically Southern in character, despite starting off as a fairly generic train-set kit. Apart from the odd criticisms on the design and original colour scheme, it is still quite an attractive model, but maybe a little over-scale.

PAGES **56–57:** *In situ at last: first on the site of the usual GWR Torpoint signal box on 'Wessex Lines', then at Sherborne and at Knighton Yard.*

completely change, or at least re-cover, the whole roof, so you will probably have to live with it.

Although there are still some elements that could do with a better solution – or perhaps some better

modelling – the overall appearance is fairly satisfying. It does at least look more like a proper signal box – albeit one of rather dubious ancestry – and less like a toy. Estimating build times can be a bit hit and miss, especially when you have to factor in planning time,

and stop to set up photographs and to type up text, but a rough estimate for the original kit and initial changes would be two evening sessions. The customizing phase actually took nearly three sessions, even when overlapping tasks, to allow paint or glue to dry properly. On balance, the extra time was well spent and involved some challenging and enjoyable modelling. The finished box would look perfectly at home on former SECR metals, even though it remains perhaps a trifle over-scale.

METCALFE

This, as is usual with Metcalfe products, is a very well designed, accurately printed and very comprehensive kit. In fact, it is virtually two kits in one, as the artwork includes both a brick and a stone version as part of the print. The instructions are well illustrated and easy to follow. The eventual model is a good representation of a medium-sized former-GWR box with a frontage of 80mm (20ft). This suggests that a frame of between fifteen and twenty levers, which is more than sufficient for most installations. The main windows have twelve panes, rather than the typical 'three-over-two' layout, indicating that the prototype is either an early version, a contractor's box or perhaps one from a smaller company absorbed into the GWR at some time on or before the 1923 grouping. With this in mind, the less common stone-built option was chosen.

There is little to be gained from a blow-by-blow account of the assembly process, as it is rare to encounter any significant difficulties with a Metcalfe kit. They go together well and the finished buildings are always as robust as they are visually satisfying. Indeed, it is more difficult to make a bad job of them than it is to get them right, as long as you are careful about your work and pay proper attention to the instructions and advice – the essence of good modelling, no matter what the task.

The main body of the kit went together in barely three hours, to the near-complete stage. The instructions were followed more or less to the letter, apart from carrying out the additional work of scribing the vertical planks. Quick-drying PVA was used for everything bar the glazing and the sequence for fixing the laser-cut timbers was slightly changed. A couple of dry runs showed that it was better, and equally accurate, to fix the gable ends first.

MODIFICATIONS

The roof could probably have been installed in the same session, but it would certainly benefit from some extra input. If it were made removable, more internal detail could be included, but this would mean re-thinking the assembly instructions. Once again,

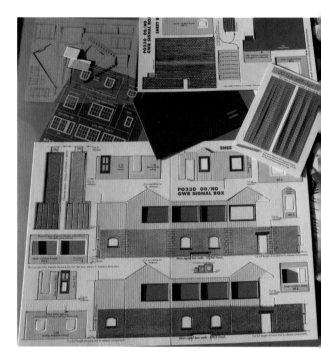

If Superquick were a step up from Bilteezi, then Metcalfe kits took everything a stage further. They are more accurate and more detailed and they benefit from improved manufacturing processes. Each component is cut with commendable precision and it could well be described as the forerunner of the newer 'etched' kits.

The stone-built GWR box (the kit also includes a brick-built option) goes together very easily and quickly, but perhaps the main timbers look a bit heavy and 'chunky' for this comparatively small version.

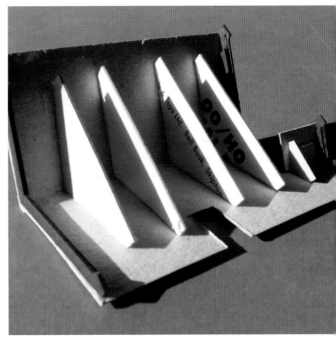

With the veranda and access stairs fitted, the model is all but ready for installation. However, the project calls for some further work to design and fit a detailed interior, together with a repaint into the original GWR colours.

The roof comes with its own reinforcing profiles and needs no additional comment if it is to be permanently fixed. Some additional reinforcing may be required if you want to keep it as a removable (but snug-fit) feature.

more time was given over to the test-fits and dry runs than to the eventual assembly. Roofs are often not quite right and this one was no exception. Just as on the previous Superquick example, it was simply too big.

The overhang along the front eaves was such that any gutters would need to be around three scale-feet out from the wall and run almost level with the tops of the windows. As modelled, the roof would also project at least half a tile beyond the barge-boards. This was better remedied now than left to become a visible irritant later. The necessary 'trims' were quickly accomplished and the barge-boards made up as sub-assemblies. In order to help the roof to maintain its shape, four formers were cut from scrap card and duly positioned. The barge-boards were then fixed to the outer edge of the roof; having first shaved its underside to a more typical thickness. As a result, the completed roof was a snug fit and quite easily detached.

A quick offer-up gives reassurance that the model will fit quite nicely into its eventual site; the apparent size and weight of those main (laser-cut) timbers is still not quite right.

The finished box stands up well to even quite close scrutiny, and it looks perfectly at home in a Western setting. Remember – this could just as easily be built with a brick base from the same kit. There is little room for improvement, and little need – this is yet another Metcalfe product that is hard to fault in either assembly or appearance. Be advised, though, that when the instructions say 'now…the really intricate bit', they are not kidding! It took three or four hours to build the stairs alone, with a bit of fiddling to get the optional walkway to fit neatly between the stairs and the lobby – but it was worth the effort in the long run.

There are a number of firms producing a whole range of corporate colours in both enamel and acrylic versions. It is generally acknowledged that the old GWR 'light and dark stone' colours (No.1 and No.3) are among the most difficult to capture with absolute accuracy. You may need to experiment, always under your layout's normal lighting, to get it right for your particular purposes.

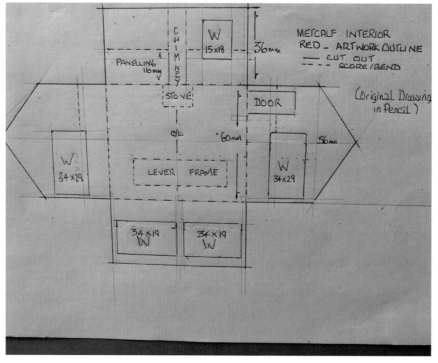

The interior is being designed to allow installation as part of the initial assembly or as a retro-fit, following the careful removal of the roof of an existing box. The first step is to draw an accurately measured flat plan on a sheet of plain paper.

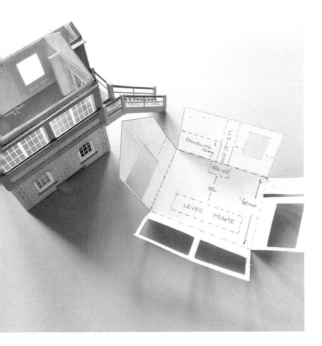

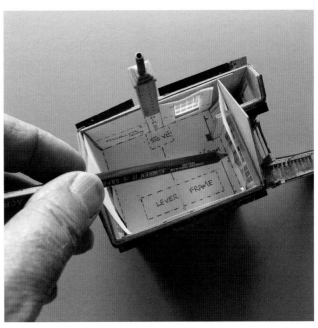

Cut out the plan, fold the walls and then test-fit it inside the box. Use your pencil to make sure it is tightly squeezed into the corners and that these inner walls match the main ones.

MAKING IMPROVEMENTS

Frankly, there is not much that could be done to improve the finished model. Metcalfe have already provided for the most significant change, by including the brick-built option within the kit itself. However, there are a few options for making your version just a bit different from all the others. As with the Superquick box, these tasks can be performed on an existing model, but it is always easier to do them before the actual assembly.

- **Wood panelling:** the print is clean and accurate, but it could be improved by carefully scoring all the joins. The back of a scalpel or craft knife is fine for the job and a 6-in steel rule is essential. Score the grooves deep enough to be worthwhile but not so deep as to scratch or tear the card. A bit of practice on some scrap (or unseen part of the kit) is always a good idea. A little judicious weathering with some pastel dust will also pay dividends.
- **Roofs:** there are two jobs that can be done here and the first is essential. Slates should really have zero thickness in this scale. Nothing can be done to the printed surfaces but it is possible to shave the

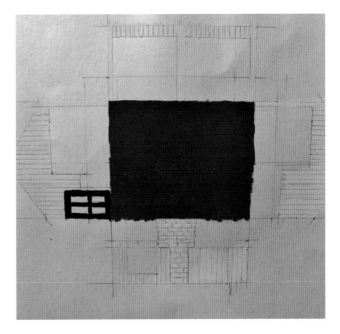

Once you are satisfied, you can begin the decorative part. The floor has been painted to resemble the traditional highly polished linoleum – a mix of BR 'bauxite' and GWR 'chocolate' enamels. The walls have also received an off-white initial coat of watercolour.

The walls can now be separated and fully worked up. The lower portion is clad with an extra layer of panels in house 'chocolate'. The upper walls can be embellished with notice-boards, pictures, calendars and anything else that might take the fancy of your resident 'bobby'.

With the fixtures and fittings ready to place, the floor and walls can be carefully fixed inside the main structure and any selected 'huminiatures' glued in position to suit the occasion you wish to represent.

A busy day in the box... and far from typical. Scenes like this would not please the purists, but they are fun to create and help to animate the layout. Just make sure you explain what everyone is doing there!

The Metcalfe box re-sited at Sherborne Tunnel and Knighton Yard. It is improved by repainting in the old GWR colours, which, if nothing else, seems to reduce the effect of those rather heavy timbers. An increased footprint is needed to accommodate the access stairs on signal boxes, particularly those that are at right-angles rather than attached to the walls.

underside of the roofs where they overhang the eaves and gable ends. Thin them as much as you can and do not forget to paint the underside with black or dark grey watercolour. The second task is down to personal choice. You may decide that the black dividing lines on Metcalfe's printed roofs are just too powerful, seemingly closer to what might be seen on a tiled roof, with its deeper shadows. The remedy is simple: cover the whole lot with a suitable tile-paper that looks more convincing. The old standby Superquick D5 Grey Tile is ideal, but there are many newer versions available as downloads.

- **Safety rail:** very few ex-GWR boxes lacked this feature. Even though most, as here, rarely had a proper veranda or walkway, the safety rail, often little more than knee-height, seemed ever present, to prevent the signalman from falling from those low sills. It is simple to make one from a length of green florist's wire, painted black before fixing.
- **Ironwork:** there are no gutters or down-pipes in the kit, not even printed ones. You can choose something from an accessory pack or fabricate the items yourself. Shown here are card gutters and florist's-wire down-pipes, painted black for quickness (check your BR(W) references to be sure).
- **Period:** as printed, the colours are correct only for the post-1948 BR era. If you are modelling the old company, you will need to repaint into 'light and dark stone', which will probably have faded over the years.
- **Missing items:** there are two missing items, one of which – the familiar GWR-style signal box name-board – is an absolute necessity. Slaters Plastic Kits do exactly the one that you need, in a pack that contains not just the board itself (which already carries the essential 'signal box' title) but also several sprues with letters of the correct size. The other omission is the distinctive roof-top ventilators, which were fitted to most boxes. They appeared as single installations on smaller boxes and whole rows on the larger types. Once again, these can be bought as accessories in either white-metal or, if you are lucky, plastic versions.

With the above points rectified, the repositioned box (even though it still lacks any interior) appears well suited to its temporary home in the West Country. As a kit, it is enjoyable and satisfying to build. The various improvements are enhancements rather than corrections, contributing to further underlining that vital GWR character. It certainly has the potential for even greater adaptation; being gable-ended rather than hipped-roofed, it lends itself nicely to being extended into a larger version. The £30 price tag for combining two kits might prove a bit steep, especially given the degree of waste from the unwanted duplicate pieces, but if you wanted a box that was suitable for a busy terminus or mainline junction, then a 'double Metcalfe' would accommodate fifty or sixty levers and would look pretty impressive.

MINOR RESERVATIONS

My only reservations relate to that laser-cut timber frame, which just seems to be too dominant; it may be that it is a tad over-scale, or perhaps the colour is too strong. It is appealing to have 'wood' representing the wood on the prototype, and it is certainly better than any pre-printed options, but somehow it fails to convince or to compare favourably with any similar photographs. It is of course a subjective view and every modeller must reach their own, equally valid, conclusion.

One other point worthy of mention, especially for those of a more purist persuasion, concerns the planking. The kit is modelled using vertical planking but on the GWR this was very much the exception, appearing nowhere in scores of Western albums; even the 'bible' (Pictorial Record of Great Western Signalling by Adrian Vaughan for OPC) yielded just one image and one works drawing. Of course there is nothing that can be done about it, so you will have to see how it all looks in the final version.

ALPHAGRAPHIX

With a comparatively low price tag, both these little Alphagraphix kits appear to be good value for money. The instructions are more than adequate and include a brief description of the prototype

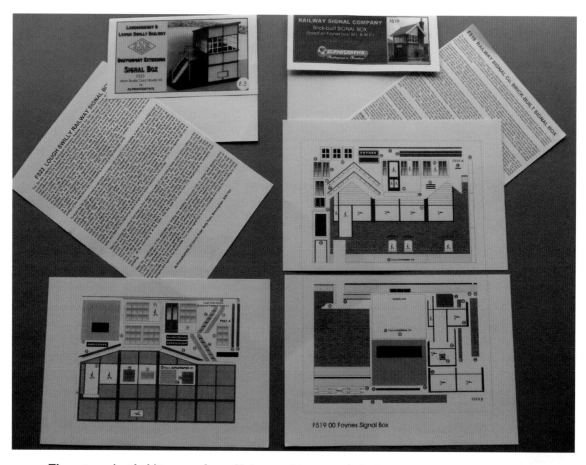

These two simple kits come from Alphagraphix, one of the longest-established and most respected names in the field of card-modelling. Their range is available only direct by mail order or, in some cases, through Freestone Models in Witney. These boxes are based on contractors' designs for long-vanished Irish railways.

and its location. There are also some guidance notes for those modellers who wish to replace the printed windows with properly glazed versions – full marks for recommending the use of a material of around 1mm thickness. The artwork is crisp and attractive and is cleverly composed to make the very best use of the small cards. Take care not to discard the pack's artwork as there are a number of components printed on the reverse! The advice to reinforce the structure should be taken as mandatory; but the customary comments to touch in the exposed edges before assembly can be more a matter of personal choice. For the record, my usual mounting board is workable (albeit a bit heavyweight for these little kits), along with some

balsa sheet of similar thickness for comparison purposes. The touching-in can be left until the building is completed, when it becomes a part of the final weathering exercise with watercolour and pastels.

These kits are really straightforward and do not need a detailed description. That said, they certainly merit, and indeed demand, proper care and attention for the best results and that means at least two or three new blades. Precision is vital on such small buildings.

NOTES ON THE BUILD

- **Preparation:** while the artwork is still in one piece, carefully remove all the door and window apertures. Next, separate all the major components

Although Alphagraphix are from across the water, they are more than suitable for any narrow-gauge or light railway anywhere in the UK. They are easy to build and would be equally easy to detail, being very similar in approach to the Bilteezi models.

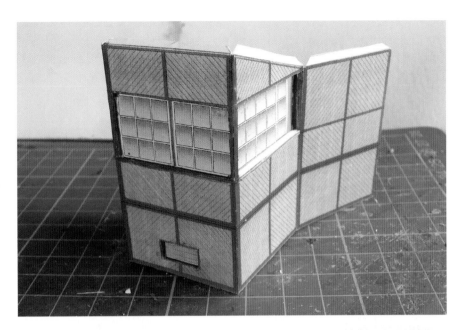

The box from Lough Swilly does not look too out of place at Watlingford on 'Wessex Lines' and is suitable for either ground or platform siting.

The second of the two kits is more familiar in the design and construction of its prototype. It could be easily taken as a British signal box from one of the smaller original companies. Using foamboard for the shell, the whole job was done in one session.

The carcass is small and easy to handle, but it is always best to introduce some bracing, a false floor and ceiling, to keep things nice and square.

that you will want to reinforce with your chosen card or balsa backing material. Group the components on to your work-piece and either mark all the apertures and outlines with a very sharp hard pencil, or pinprick them with a needle and then join the dots. Cut the openings first and then separate the main items.

• **Corner joints:** decide whether to form the crucial (and perpetually difficult) corners by the score-and-bend method or by the simpler butt-joints, and cut or score as required. On this example, the second method was chosen; the front wall backing was cut to full width, the two side walls were reduced at the front by one thickness of card and the rear wall was reduced by two thicknesses to fit in between them.

- **Assembly:** take your time over this, ensuring that you offer up as often as necessary. You may need to carry out some slight trimming to get all four backing pieces to fit nicely together, with the window uprights probably giving the worst headache. Be careful with the adhesive, as soggy card is easily stretched or torn; also remember that virtually all card is a series of laminations, and the window uprights, being scarcely a millimetre wide, may well start to disintegrate as you work. Balsa wood, cut with the grain, might prove a better alternative. Both materials are inexpensive so you can afford to experiment.

- **Windows:** cut these from the artwork and strengthen them with a couple of extra thicknesses cut from the spare areas of the sheet. Because you have, by using this backing material, effectively reduced the inside dimensions you will need to trim the outer ends of the windows to fit the smaller space. Once again, it is a matter of offering up, and trimming little and often, to get all three windows ready to fix. Be sparing with the glue and do not press too firmly until they are all evenly placed and properly upright.

- **Staircases:** treat these as you would the windows and any timber overlays; remove the unwanted centres first, taking great care not to cause 'collateral damage' to the delicate posts and rails. In the case of the larger Foynes signal box do read the instructions and relate them to your finished model. It is too easy to miss something and combine the various components incorrectly. Unfortunately, the pack shot illustration does not show the entrance end of the building, so you may need to search online to find a clear reference.

- **Completion:** you can now safely continue the detailing as set out on the instruction sheet. Some of the remaining components are very small and delicate, demanding the sharpest blade and very careful use of your chosen glue. The tiniest amount, applied with a cocktail stick, should give the desired result. You can now carry out the postponed touch-

The staircase is no more difficult than any other and repays the extra care taken in cutting out and gluing.

ing-in of all the exposed edges with the appropriate watercolours. The printed windows were given a light brush coating with Deluxe Glue 'n' Glaze, with the result that they now resemble frosted glass!

CONCLUSIONS

Both the Alphagraphix signal boxes would look quite at home on any narrow-gauge or light-railway layout, as well as within their intended Irish settings. Should you want to use them on a Big Four or BR layout, then some judicious repainting with the correct house colour(s) will produce the necessary transformation.

Alphagraphix seems to be one of the unsung heroes in the field of card kits, offering a vast range of models to the discerning builder. They are well worth investigating, as they are modestly priced and the end results can be quite impressive, with a bit of extra care and patience.

ABOVE, LEFT AND RIGHT: *The actual box has survived into preservation (albeit with some more recent changes). The original as modelled would be easy to upgrade with glazed windows and detailed interior.*

LEFT AND OPPOSITE: *Foynes box, re-located to deepest Wessex, once again shows how its compact design will suit both off- and on-platform locations.*

LAST WORD

It would have been good to include an example of the former Prototype range, but, as they currently owe their existence to Freestone Models, and are still some way from being made fully available, this would have been unwise. They remain, however, the very zenith of the card-kit industry, combining the ultimate in accuracy with some outstanding printing and clever kit design. They were not beginner's kits – nor were they intended to be – but they did present a worthwhile but never unsurmountable challenge to the modeller in search of lineside realism. If you are fortunate enough to come across a kit that is appropriate for your layout, perhaps at a toy fair or auction, do buy it and try it.

PAGES **72–73:**
*Examples from
'Wessex Lines',
featuring the
Prototype GWR,
LSWR and LMS kits.
Sadly, the supply
of kits has dried up
since the company
ceased trading
(although Freestone
Models are striving
to re-introduce
them). These were at
the absolute zenith
of card-kit design
and manufacture,
beautifully printed
and dimensionally
100 per cent.*

CHAPTER FOUR

ASSEMBLING AND IMPROVING PLASTIC KITS

OPTIONS

For old hands who have been plying their trade for more years than they care to remember, plastic signal-box kits have always meant the ubiquitous Airfix versions. Ubiquitous because, despite undoubtedly Midland origins, they could be endlessly tweaked and installed on layouts covering every BR region. In more recent years, the Kitmaster range, produced by Dapol, has done a sterling job in keeping both the products and the original Airfix branding alive and well.

Another long-established company, with a well-deserved reputation for both accuracy and quality, is Ratio. Their extensive ranges cover the whole gamut, from builder's aids to lineside accessories, rolling stock and buildings, including signal boxes. Their kits make up into perfect scale models of identifiable prototypes and are more than capable of holding their own, even on the most discerning of layouts. It is to Ratio's credit that they maintain high standards in kits that, while not cheap, are neither over-expensive nor difficult to construct. They are comfortably within the skills of the novice kit-builder and, while they do repay a little extra time and effort, no one need be in any way over-awed by them. The current catalogue shows that they have four kits available. Three are firmly GWR; with ground-level and platform-level versions of the Mackenzie & Holland type (from Highley on the SVR), and a newer model of the standard brick-built type found all over the system. The fourth kit is a distinctly Midland box, not unlike an upmarket interpretation of the old Airfix version. Prices do vary, but currently range from around £17.00 to £23.00.

More recently, the name of Wills Kits has become synonymous with plastic kits and bits. Their already extensive range seems to grow almost month by month, to the extent that it has a number of books dedicated to helping modellers to get the best from these well-engineered products. Unlike the old Airfix model, which could best be described as a fairly typical Midland box, the Wills Scenic Series kit is a commendably accurate version of a Saxby & Farmer gable-end box found all over the system. This contractor was providing boxes and designs to a large number of the original pre-grouping companies, so yet again that word 'ubiquitous' is easily justified. With a simple change of colour scheme, the box would be quite appropriate from Wales to the Wash and from Dover to Doncaster.

A more recent addition to the dealers' shelves comes from a company that is already a household name for most modellers. As well as being a major retail outlet, with over-the-counter, mail-order and online shopping, Gaugemaster is also synonymous with control systems and other electronic products. Their Fordhampton range of 4mm railway buildings (doubtless named after their HQ in the former goods shed at Ford station, but bearing distinct overtones of the foreign GWR structures) now includes a signal-box kit. It is a well-crafted version of a standard Western timber-framed, hipped-roof box and is an interesting alternative to the Prototype card version – but it does come in distinctly Southern colours.

DAPOL/KITMASTER

Dapol's kit comes in the usual polythene envelope together with a simple, easy-to-follow sheet of instructions. Although the design is around fifty years old and was originally aimed at the toy market and general modeller rather than today's demanding clientele, the mouldings remain crisp, clean and rela-

The ever-popular Kitmaster/Airfix/ Dapol has been around since the latter days of steam on BR. Although originally aimed at the train-set market, it has stood the test of time and its sound basic design makes it a good subject for customizing and detailing.

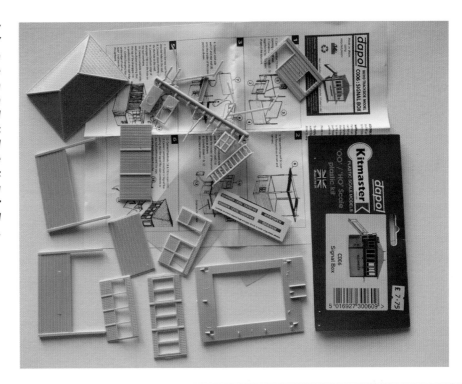

tively flash-free. Dapol continue to use all the original tooling and the result belies the age and the huge numbers of kits they have delivered.

The kit comprises the eight frets that make up the walls and the glazed first floor; the one-piece hipped roof section; the veranda and a final sprue for the door, window and other fittings. There is also a sheet of glazing material, optional name transfers and a comprehensive instruction-sheet. There is no 'floor' provided so this would need to be included in the task-list for anyone wishing to model the interior.

The instructions and its exploded diagrams make the assembly process a quite straightforward exercise; however you will need to source your own prototype-information for colour schemes and accurate detailing. The recommended adhesive is liquid-poly applied with a small fine brush and this is quite in keeping with a kit of this quality. You could of course assemble it exactly as bought, but this kit has the potential to be lifted well beyond its 'toy' status. The enhancements are all relatively straightforward and need only the odd extra tool and some suitable references. They could be applied retrospectively but I chose to incorporate them into the main assembly

Regardless of how much or how little further improvement is planned, some initial work is always needed. The top priority is to slim down all the window frames; a good reference image is helpful.

sequence. As in the previous examples I stuck to the instructions and the whole thing went together very easily: but I did choose to leave the painting (except the interior) until the box was completed. This did make it a little more difficult, but it proved the point that a finished item could be 're-cycled' and used a new layout representing a different region.

MAKING IMPROVEMENTS

A number of improvements were made to the kit, but you need not limit yourself to the additional work described here. Reference to various sources of images, such as Settle & Carlisle Steam Finale (Welch/Runpast) and Rails in The Fells (Jenkinson/ PECO), and an online search for 'Midland Railway signal boxes', should yield more than enough different interpretations for even the most diligent modeller.

- **Glazing:** as supplied, all the main windows are simply one whole pane of 'glass'; in reality, these should be made up of six individual panes, together with their glazing bars. The small window next to the door is correct with its four panes, but the glazing bars are far too thick. To remedy this, carve away any over-scale woodwork and then either fabricate new windows from the supplied plastic sheet; alternatively, if you are lucky, you may be able to locate something suitable from the pre-printed ranges.

- **Safety rails:** these are essential for the veranda and can be quickly made from the usual 0.020in micro-rod. You will need a simple pin vice and suitable drill bit for this.
- **Roof:** as is common with plastic kits, the slates are too pronounced and more like tiles than ultra-thin slates. There are several options: either patiently sand down the unwanted relief detail, or carefully scrape it away using the flat of a scalpel. Alternatively, cover the whole lot with tile paper, or simply choose to live with it.

Since this style of box was widely used across the whole of the former Midland Railway (and elsewhere), and since it can adapt to its location as quickly as its colour scheme can be changed, there is nothing to be gained by discussing any extensive customizing. The plain-glass effect from the lack of individual panes may be answered by replacing with something regionally appropriate. The addition of valancing can be another simple act of 'regionalization', as on my Sherborne version. (Incidentally, this particular item is none other than that first original Airfix box, now over fifty years old. It has been on no fewer than six previous layouts.)

The various enhancements are all quite simple to carry out and require little in the way of special skills. They do, however, call for a modicum of care and a significant amount of patience – an essential attribute of every modeller!

Slimming down the frames is a fairly tedious task requiring care and patience rather than any great skill. Little and often is the answer for the scalpel work.

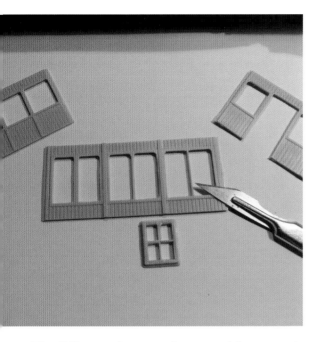

The difference between the treated frames and the originals becomes more apparent as the work progresses.

The end of a steel rule is useful to ensure neat and square corners. Tube cement rather than liquid poly gives a little extra time for adjustments while it sets.

When the basic shell is firmly cemented, and having previously sketched out your plans for the interior, you can add your artwork to the walls. Any furniture, fixtures and fittings that will be close to or fixed to the walls can also be added; use the 'step' as part of the eventual floor.

ABOVE LEFT AND RIGHT: *The central area of the operating floor can now be put together as a fully finished sub-assembly and huminiatures added if you wish. Essential items include the lever frame, instrument shelf and diagram. The 'fat controller' is an S & T Inspector paying his annual visit!*

All the various items are now ready to be permanently assembled into a detailed version of this vintage plastic kit.

The safety rails around the veranda are not only an essential addition, they also add a nice finishing touch. Black micro-rod would have saved a rather tricky paint job, but at least the white version is effective in the photograph.

FURTHER ADVICE

There are a number of points worth considering, although you may not encounter these particular issues. Watch out for warping; the plastic used is on the soft side, and shipping and storage may well have distorted some components. Gentle hand pressure and flexing will usually rectify the problem. The roof may be a particular weak point in this respect, so double-check it before fixing. When drilling the holes for stanchions to support the guard rails, always do them prior to assembly and work from the underside of the veranda. The access stairs can be a bit tricky so be prepared to devise your own sequence to make them secure and square.

Finally, the large expanse of windows produces a well-lit and very empty interior. A false floor is the least you can get away with, but a detailed interior is a definite 'plus', although there are some potential problems.

Those modellers who want to relocate the box in GWR territory will not only have to impose the

The finished Midland signal box would be a must-have for anyone modelling the much-loved Settle and Carlisle line, but it would not be out of place further south and with some careful customizing it could turn up where least expected.

ABOVE LEFT AND RIGHT: *The increasingly familiar photo site at Knighton Yard puts this vintage kit into a layout setting on 'Wessex Lines'. Incidentally, the 8F is probably the more at home as it represents a Swindon-built example that lingered on the GWR after the war.*

That Airfix kit from 1966, fifty years on. In the interim, it has been on five layouts, had three rebuilds and carried four colour schemes. It now sits on the columns from the Airfix water tower as Sherborne 'A' box – that was a shilling and sixpence well spent!

correct colour scheme, but also change the name-board. GWR differed in this, as it did in almost everything else, always having its name-boards on the front of the box, facing the tracks, and never on the gable ends. It was also the only company always to add the words 'SIGNAL BOX' to the location. The Slaters 3mm lettering pack includes scale name-boards with those words already in place; all you have to do is add an appropriate place name.

RATIO

Ratio's vast experience across a whole range of plastic kits and accessories makes them past masters at design, precision manufacturing and ease of assembly, and their kits are as easy to describe as they are to execute. Simply follow the instructions for the box or boxes of your choice. There are less expensive kits around but few can match the accuracy of fit that you get from Ratio. The company also produces high-quality wagon and carriage kits that make up into finely detailed and free-running stock.

There is little that you need to do during assembly process, except to take the time and trouble to the kit justice. If you intend to fit a detailed interior, also

Two of the signal boxes from Ratio's current range. They are both based on the version, still in existence at Highley on the Severn Valley Railway, that was originally built by contractors for the GWR. The smaller model is well suited to an installation on a platform, but it can also be sited at ground level.

The roofs have been modelled as detachable in order to detail the interiors at a later date. The makers have included a printed back wall, which features the small kitchen range and proper chimney typical of this type of box.

The larger of the two Ratio GWR boxes represents Sherborne Tunnel box on 'Wessex Lines'.

In the opposite corner of the loft, the smaller Ratio version serves as Winterbourne box and is quite at home at ground level.

available from Ratio, you will find that there is pre-printed back wall ready to fix in place. It would be a good idea to take advantage of the sliding-window option and model them open, so that the inside can be seen more easily. The small six-pane windows inevitably restrict the view. Beyond that, all you need to consider are the final colour scheme, the name-boards and any minor changes if your model is to be based on an actual location; in such cases, it is essential to refer to some good colour images.

WILLS SCENICS

Wills is a major name in the field of plastic build-ings, accessories and builder's aids. This kit comes as a boxed item, in common with the many other offerings in Wills' extensive range. The first point to note is the very wise decision to work in plain white plastic. This can effectively remove the need for any interior painting and, more importantly, even the window frames and glazing bars may be left alone. The second point is how far plastic technology has progressed in the post-Airfix/Kitmaster decades.

This is clearly a model aimed at the enthusiast rather than the toy market. The mouldings are crisp and clean and detail is much finer. The kit is more comprehensive, but this is reflected in the price of around £11.00, around 70 per cent more than the Dapol version. The instruction sheet is easy to follow and gives guidance on how to alter the model using the included optional items. There is also some useful prototype information but it should not be taken too literally. Saxby & Farmer supplied so many different pre-grouping companies, each with their own house styles, that no two boxes appear identical. If you intend your box to represent a particular company or specific example, do some online research before you begin the assembly. You may well find that there are some minor, but none the less obvious, variations that require attention. It is worth taking special note in respect of the window design: the model comes with a nine-pane sliding type and a quick trawl through the available images throws up no examples of this.

The assembly process for the Wills kit is quite straightforward and requires little extra comment.

The signal box from Wills Scenics is based, like the Ratio kits, on a real prototype. This is another example of a contractor's design, in this case by Saxby & Farmer, and could be authentically sited almost anywhere in the country. The use of white plastic for the main mouldings means that, at a pinch, the glazing bars might not need to be painted.

The notes advise you to carry out much of the painting before assembling. The usual recommendations – paint the interior first, and definitely do the glazing bars before attaching the 'glass' – certainly apply. In fact, this is one case where you may choose to leave the windows as plain white plastic.

The reduction in the thickness of the slates is unavoidable. It is laborious work with the scalpel, scraping away the detail until the surface is virtually flat. One roof section is untouched and the other is nearing completion.

The box visually complete, with whitewashed lower windows on the ground floor. This was fairly common practice and at least gave some privacy to the quite valuable wires and switch-gear located within.

The plan was to model a box with a fully detailed and removable operating floor, which was also accessible via a detachable 'press-fit' rear wall.

IMPROVING THE ROOF

The only significant shortcoming relates to the roof – again. Getting the roof right on any model is so important, because, unlike in real life, it will invariably be viewed from above. The individual slates on this kit are so deeply moulded that they resemble the clay tiles found on barns or period cottages (and even for that application they are too pronounced and too regular to be convincing). There is no reference to a Saxby box that featured anything other than normal slates, so it does need some attention.

For the record, each roof section took over an hour of scraping with a scalpel, trying to eradicate the scale inch-deep gaps between the slates. If you do decide that the exercise is worthwhile, the best method is as follows: place the roof section on a sheet of paper on a good, solid work surface; use a fresh blade and grip the scalpel as close to the blade as possible; working up the roof, scrape row by row to reduce the vertical gaps between the tiles, dealing with only a couple of tiles at a time; finally, draw the flat blade diagonally and vertically across the whole piece to reduce the steps between the rows. Repeat as necessary'!

FINISHING

With the roof modifications out of the way, the rest is plain sailing and the final product is well up to the high standards of this deservedly popular range of kits. There are some tricky bits, but nothing that should prove too taxing, even for a first-time modeller. It is simply a question of following the instructions, taking your time and offering up the pieces to check for fit before gluing. Perhaps the most difficult areas are the half-roofs and ridge-tiling, the gutters and finally the veranda. Do not despair if things do go wrong – immediate dismantling is fairly easy with some extra solvent and careful prising apart with a scalpel. It may take you more than one attempt before you get the roof looking right from every angle.

It is certainly worth a bit of extra time to install a suggestion of interior detail, but you need not go

ABOVE LEFT AND RIGHT: *A couple of close-ups of the interior as viewed from the back. It is easy to imagine a modeller proudly demonstrating this level of detail to an exhibition visitor.*

The interior is still quite impressive from the normal viewing angle. The paintwork is deliberately faded to give the impression of a workaday box in need of some exterior TLC. The improved view of the interior is gained through the open window.

The Wills Scenics box now takes its turn at Knighton Yard; as it is a contractor-built structure, a fresh paint job could re-locate it almost anywhere in the UK.

too far, as it is quite difficult to make the two-piece hipped roof detachable. Only model those items that may be glimpsed through the windows (see Chapter 2). The other option is to go for a fully detailed interior but to make the rear wall detachable rather than the roof; in this way, the whole floor can be withdrawn for viewing, or indeed for any subsequent improvements.

GAUGEMASTER

Gaugemaster's Fordhampton signal box is a little bit quirky. It is obviously intended for use on Southern Railway layouts, hence the colours of the mouldings and the pack shot; not to mention the designs of the complementary stickers and transfers, but the prototype is clearly of GWR origins, right down to the unmistakable 'three-over-two' five-pane windows. To confuse matters still further, the name transfers include the words 'SIGNAL BOX' – another GWR peculiarity. Then there is that mysterious console moulded as part of the operating floor – has this steam-era mechanical box suddenly entered the world of electrical switching? One of the more posi-

tive aspects of the kit relates to its overall footprint. The chosen prototype has an internal staircase. This eliminates a tricky bit of modelling and, more importantly, it keeps the length to the basic 3¾in (95mm), saving some 2in (50mm) against an external staircase version.

The model has been manufactured for Gaugemaster by no less a name than Faller, one of the legends of the European scene. It is hardly a surprise, then, that the kit design and quality are of the highest order. One approach is to ignore any Southern pretentions and accept the kit as an excellent solution to the need for a medium-sized GWR/BR(W) signal box. Whichever choice you make, the use of dark green plastic for the main walls demands that the modeller

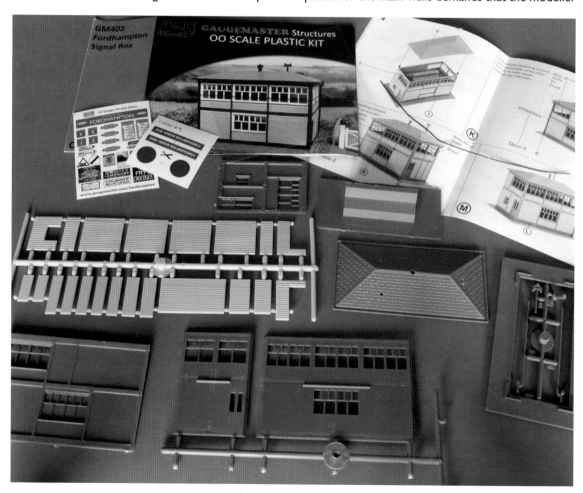

The fairly recent addition to Gaugemaster's Fordhampton range, designed and manufactured by Faller GmbH. and of a high quality... albeit with a rather dubious prototype ancestry.

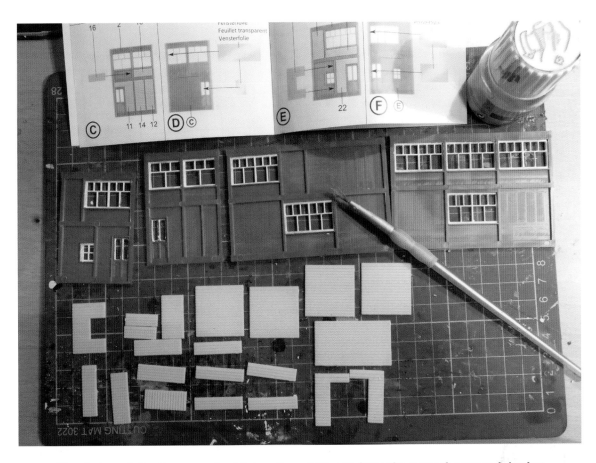

The design of the Gaugemaster kit is rather different from the normal approach in that all the wood panels are supplied as separate mouldings to be fixed between the raised timbers on the walls. It seems sensible to cut all of them out in one go and apply them in one batch operation. The green plastic window frames and glazing bars have already been painted white and the panels have also been treated.

white-paint all the window frames, glazing bars and the interior of the operating floor. Even if you plan to stay with the quasi-Southern version, the only green bits to remain visible should be the doors and main timbers. A GWR version will in any case require a total paint job.

AN ALTERNATIVE ASSEMBLY SEQUENCE

My own approach to the build process departed quite significantly from the instructions, which are somewhat sketchy. Having studied the various components, it seemed easier and quicker to tackle the four walls simultaneously rather than sequentially, as shown in the notes, so the first

move was to separate all the cream panels and the walls from their sprues.

- **Painting:** first, paint all the window frames and glazing bars with white enamel. Matt is best for this sort of job, but you may wish to go for satin or even a full gloss finish; it is down to personal choice. It is also open to debate whether to paint the inside of the bars before fixing the glazing material. On the one hand, it is certainly easier at this stage; the downsides are that too much paint may get in the way of properly securing the 'glass', and the final appearance of the interior will look less realistic.

- **Walls:** place the walls on the bench and sort the panels into their various groups. This is an

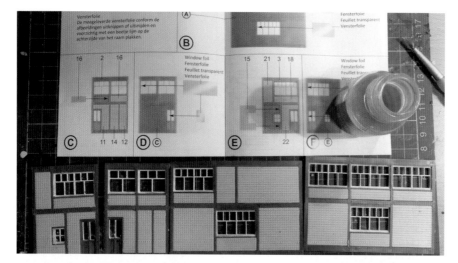

The task of fitting the panels is easy; pre-sort them into groups by their respective sizes and fix them with a fairly liberal brushing of liquid-poly.

The design of the operating floor rules out any interior detailing. However, you should still whitewash the walls and apply the proper house-colour green to the timbers.

opportune time to check you have them all the right way up! It is then a quick and simple exercise to brush liquid-poly into each recess and press home the appropriate panel. With all the pieces laid out in front of you, mistakes are eliminated and multiple handling is avoided. It took less than five minutes to have all the walls finished.

- **Glazing:** next comes the fixing of the glazing material. A word of advice here: the sheet supplied with the kit is very thin (barely 0.03mm), making it more difficult to fix and more prone to bowing and distortion. A quick rummage in the spares box soon located a leftover sheet from another kit that was five times thicker, at 0.15mm, and made a far better alternative. Cut

and fix with cement or liquid-poly; use enough to really soften the walls but not so much as to risk it squeezing out on to the window panes. Press each piece down firmly with flat of your scalpel; avoid using your fingertip, as that is a sure-fire way of causing smears.

- **Interior:** finally, it is time to whitewash the interior of the operating floor and pick out the insides of the glazing bars. This is not the easiest of tasks, so take your time and keep the windows – and your hands – steady. Try to cover as much of the visible green plastic as you can and do not worry if you stray on to the actual panes, as it is easy to tidy things up with a cocktail stick or sharpened matchstick.

The finished box is attractive enough in its Southern livery, but the five-pane 'three-over-two' windows simply scream Great Western. A total repaint would produce a more suitable and authentic end result.

Any attempt at interior detailing has been ignored at this time. The answer would be to treat it in exactly the same way as the Dapol exercise and create a complete sub-assembly to replace the existing floor moulding.

'RE-REGIONALIZING'

The finished signal box is shown in its Southern livery as intended by Gaugemaster (Humbrol 113 Stock Green/Gloy ST G 14 Buff), and, perhaps more accurately, in GWR colours (Railmatch Light Stone/ Precision P22 Dark Stone) and with appropriate renaming. The GWR paints are not entirely satisfactory in terms of their tonal qualities. They lack the warmth of the colours that have been faithfully reproduced on the preserved lines – a glance at the recent photographs on the West Somerset (see Chapter 7, on scratch-building) will prove the point. Keen GWR modellers may well wish to shop around in search of a closer match.

There are two final points to remember. First, those original paints were lead-based and tended to fade quite quickly, so the addition of some matt white

Just to prove the point of the origins of Fordhampton box, this is the fairly convincing result of a repaint and a new name-board and a subsequent re-siting to the coast of Glorious Devon. The boxes with ground-floor access only are much easier to site on a layout than those with external stairs.

will help towards greater realism. Second, those who are modelling the BR(W) era should of course apply the familiar chocolate and cream colour scheme.

The smallest of signal boxes are often not boxes at all. This is a recent addition to the range from Wills Scenics and comprises no fewer than four ground frames: one pair of the four-lever type, complete with an instrument shelf, and another pair of the simpler two-lever type.

All things considered, this recent addition to the selection of 'Western' signal boxes is a welcome one and seems certain to find favour among the many aficionados of God's Wonderful Railway.

WILLS SCENICS LEVER/ GROUND FRAME

This is just about as small as you can go in the realm of signal boxes. This sort of structure was located anywhere that required points or crossings that could not be effectively operated from the nearest proper box. The kit, like the real thing, is very simple and includes two sets of frames, each consisting of a four-lever and a two-lever version. There is also a representation of the block instrument board, which enabled the local man to stay in touch with the controlling box for that section. The instructions are equally simple, but do offer suggested colour schemes for the levers. Since there is a choice, one set will be painted and detailed specifically to operate a level-crossing, and incorporated into a setting in a later chapter.

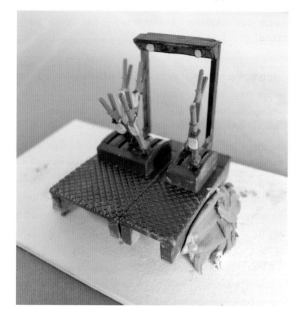

A four-lever and two-lever combined, perhaps to control a distant goods loop. There are two sets for facing points with black levers correctly governed by interlocking mechanisms and their blue levers. The two red levers control the protecting home/stop signals.

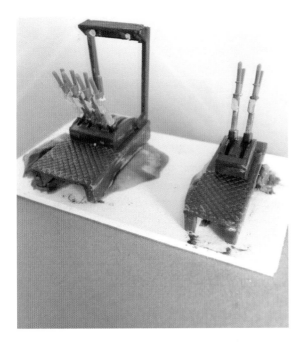

This second example should, by rights, be found at a level-crossing. The four-lever frame operates the protecting 'up' and 'down' distant and home signals, while the two brown levers operate the locking mechanisms for the actual gates.

In some cases, the ground frames were given a somewhat primitive hut for shelter. This is one the versions included on the Bilteezi sheet. Some frames were also given official name-boards and these were by no means confined only to the hutted versions.

It is worth remembering that in many instances the simple ground frames were given a proper little shed for protection – and were immediately promoted to the role of 'signal box', complete with name-board. In other cases, a rudimentary tin shelter might be provided, but many others remained open to the elements. The practice of naming these remote frames was not universal, but it was certainly quite common and you would be perfectly justified in giving your own model(s) a correctly styled name-board. (See the example in the Bilteezi section of Chapter 3.)

Assembly of the four little frames is quite straightforward and requires very few words of extra advice. There are a number of tips that might help, however:

- Like the signals or crossings they control, these features are on permanent view, so it is worth taking due care over their construction and painting, including any extra details you may add.
- When you fix the signal levers, make sure that their positions correspond with the aspects displayed on the signals themselves. If the levers have been pulled forward, then your signals must be 'off' and the gates closed to road traffic. This would be my personal choice.
- The kits are actually a bit 'fiddly' to assemble and it may make things a little easier if you put the frames on to temporary card-bases. They can be held in place with a dab of Blu-tack or Plasticine.

CHAPTER FIVE

DEALING WITH DOWNLOAD KITS

INTRODUCTION

The idea of buying a model kit online is nothing new today and there are doubtless hundreds of modellers who have done it. Probably less familiar is the idea of having a kit delivered, not to your doorstep, but to your laptop. To those who come from the generation before TV, before phones in the home never mind in the pocket, and before the demise of steam and Hornby clockwork, the developments in computer technology defy belief. No sooner had we got to grips with CAD/CAM, digital control and sound simulation than along came the reality of designing, marketing, selling and delivering kits all around the world from one terminal to another. At the moment it has only reached the stage of two-dimensional items but, before long, home printers will be able to produce a fully three-dimensional kit, including motor, gearbox, wheels and motion.

Those modellers who have yet to encounter their first download need not be concerned. The basic principles are the same as any other kit build; the difference lies in the concept itself and the extra time and effort required, although this is more than compensated for by the low cost and free repeats. There is no need for any advanced technology – an average laptop will be fine and home printers are not prohibitively expensive. Multi-page files for large and complicated buildings can be printed in minutes and the production of single-sheet reprints is almost instant.

The quality of the kits appears to be at least as good as that of the current card kits available on the high street, although it has not been possible to road-test every available product. As long as your printer is performing correctly, the colours are prototypically accurate, well defined and well registered. The accompanying instructions are easy to follow and comprehensive; they are also augmented by helpful notes on the actual artwork. Taken simply as the starting points, there is nothing either present or missing that might prevent the modeller from obtaining the optimum results.

TOOLS AND MATERIALS

THE TOOL-BOX

As with every kit or scratch-build that you assemble, it is up to you, but the tool-box remains little changed from that needed when assembling card kits. This includes a scalpel and 10a blade(s), or craft knife if preferred, scissors, a heavier blade for the thicker versions of reinforcing card, glue pen(s) and glue-stick(s), a tube of clear/universal glue, various sizes of bulldog clips, and a decent cutting mat and a good light. The smaller tubes of clear glue as are easier to handle and less prone to overflowing. Glue-sticks tend to 'grab' and are almost dry within seconds – basic paper glue and paper paste, applied sparingly with a larger watercolour brush, can make acceptable substitutes. The most important 'tools' are those that should already be inherent in every enthusiastic modeller, namely, patience and the persistence to complete the project.

PAPER, CARD, BOARD AND WOOD

In respect of the materials required, the first and most obvious is a good-quality copier paper, of at least 80gsm (or, even better, 100gsm). This should give an excellent result and is unlikely to jam your printer when you are dealing with multi-page runs. If you intend to make extensive use of downloads, it is worth including some transparent sheets for the window glazing in your stock list. It is not easy to recommend a particular type, since the choice will depend on your printer. Seek technical advice on the thickest you can use without difficulty or damage. Inks should not be a problem, but some brands may appear shinier than others; this is not the end of the world, however, as a quick waft of Water Colour Matt Varnish will resolve the problem. (Indeed, many off-the-shelf kits suffer from this effect, which can be cured the same way).

You will also need to have ready adequate stocks of various thicknesses of card. Each kit designer will make their own recommendations on what is best in order to obtain the optimum results. If you can source card(s) exactly in line with their advice, this is clearly the way to go, but it may not be that easy. Kit designers will probably give card thicknesses in millimetres, while local art or hobby shops are more likely to stock it by weight (gsm). One solution is to adhere to the specification and buy your supplies direct from the kit's recommended supplier. Alternatively, purchase a cheap digital Vernier scale and measure what is on offer from local craft shops or even from recycled packaging. If you cannot get an exact match, it is better to use extra layers of thinner card rather than using something that is too thick. Heavier weights of drawing paper often equate with the thinner cards, but avoid those with rippled or textured surfaces. The right card is the foundation upon which your download artwork will be built.

As an alternative to card, you could try balsa-wood sheets. Most model shops offer a fairly good selection in the normal sheet size of 4 x 36in (100 x 900mm). However, the thickness may be defined either in Imperial (1/16th, 1/32nd, 3/32nd, and so on), or in metric (0.3mm, 0.5mm, 1.5mm, and so on). Balsa-wood sheets have their advantages and disadvantages when compared with the mostly commonly used card, mounting board or, as it is sometimes called, art board. It is about three times more expensive per square foot, but you can buy it in smaller quantities, which makes it easier to handle and to store. It is easier to cut and to work with and is equally robust when used properly. It is definitely lighter in weight than card, yet it is just as durable. (On the snow-covered village of Winterbourne on 'Wessex Lines',

which was constructed for an exhibition in 1973 and has survived three loft layouts and a house move, all the buildings have balsa shells.) Unlike the board, it is not a laminate, so there is little risk of disintegration even when it is used in small sections. It is easy to fix with any of the usual glues and of course balsa cement is perfect when joining wood-to-wood.

One downside is that when it is used for walls with the grain vertical (ideal for very small window uprights), it will need some lateral bracing, to prevent any bowing or warping across the grain.

If you have not tried it before, give it a go; you may well be favourably surprised by how effective it is.

MARKET DEVELOPMENTS AND POINTS TO CONSIDER

The download section of the market is expanding quickly. The hobby has always supported a healthy 'cottage industry' of small manufacturers, often just a one-man band, producing those little extras and accessories to transform and personalize kits, r-t-r models and scenery. In the past, these items often came as white-metal castings, and were the result of quite considerable inputs of skill, time and money. Inevitably, although some small companies flourished, many others lost their market due to the ever-improving r-t-r products. Rapid developments in computer technology have significantly reduced the need for traditional manufacturing methods, particularly as used by the small-scale garden-shed enterprises.

Today's entrepreneurs still need the skill to identify potential markets and the ability to devise and design products to meet demand, but from there on it is more about artistry than engineering. The home computer has effectively replaced the factory in the shed. What better area to exploit than the field of architectural modelling, where virtually every component, irrespective of the eventual medium, can start life as a piece of inexpensive two-dimensional artwork? All that is needed is to simply bring that artwork up to an acceptable standard, deliver it straight to the modeller's work-bench and then let them do the rest.

With new enterprises being launched every month – or so it seems – it is impossible to carry out a fully comprehensive review. In the time it takes to progress any work from laptop to bookshelf, many new kits will have come on to the market and others may have been withdrawn or replaced. What follows is simply a representative selection from the market at the time of writing; needless to say, the usual advice applies: do your own thorough search before buying.

The following points for consideration apply to any download kit:

• **Card backing sheets:** most downloads imply that the complete printed sheets should be glued direct on to the appropriate thickness of card. This is somewhat cumbersome, as well as being less than efficient, as it is a near impossibility to ensure that each component receives the same amount of glue and is therefore securely and completely stuck to the card. Roughly separating the various items and then fixing them individually (and more compactly grouped) on to several smaller card work-pieces more or less guarantees secure fixing and makes for much easier handling.

• **Apertures:** there are inevitably many apertures to be cut out, no matter what kit you are building. Many of these, especially around the windows, require you to leave just a few millimetres of 'frame' surrounding the hole. This creates an unnecessary degree of risk and fragility, which is easily avoided if you cut the apertures while the work-piece is whole, rather than attempting to cut them from the already separated component.

• **Window glazing:** if you are unable to source any suitable film for your printer, or you simply wish to explore alternative methods, there are several options: (a) check your local stockist or online for an appropriate pre-printed version; (b) it is tricky and laborious, but it is possible (just) to carefully cut out the window frames and glazing bars from the download artwork, then glue this delicate fret to the glazing of your choice; (c) if you are a glutton for punishment, then tape your glazing over the artwork and build up the frames and bars with strips from self-adhesive labels; (d) as above, tape your glazing material over the artwork and then with a ruler and pen simply trace the outlines on to surface. If the frames and bars are black, any fine-tip marker pen or even the finest ballpoint will do the job. If they are white, a gel pen or mapping pen/ drawing ink will be equally suitable. This is possibly the easiest option.

THE SCALESCENES SIGNAL BOX

When looking for a kit that was neither too simple, which might make it all seem too easy, nor too complicated, which might make it seem too difficult or time-consuming, the Scalescenes GWR signal box was just right. John Wiffen's designs were the first to appear in the mainstream market and his current range (which numbers over fifty) is certainly the largest of all; the kits are exceptionally well thought out and the artwork is excellent. They are well within the capabilities of the average first-time builder and, as the model is a GWR version, it is ideal to compare with other interpretations. (For reviews of a couple of John Wiffen's other designs – his North-Light Engine Shed and very impressive Coal Stage – see *Modelling Engine Sheds and Motive Power Depots*, from the Crowood Press.)

Once you have invested £4.99 for the GWR signal box kit ref. R010, your printer will produce one file that contains the four A4 pages of assembly instructions and general tips, and another with four further pages of the kit itself. Although this is one of earlier introductions in the Scalescenes range (from around 2005), it has been recently revamped. It is undoubtedly 'Western', but it does come with some regional variations for the colour schemes applied to the paintwork on the doors and barge-boards. There is an attractively finished interior for the operating floor for those who wish to go the extra mile and install a detailed interior.

The kit does require you to cut out the individual windows, but it also offers the choice of some specially commissioned etches from Brassmasters. This option includes the earlier-pattern window frames, levers and handrails and is also available with the

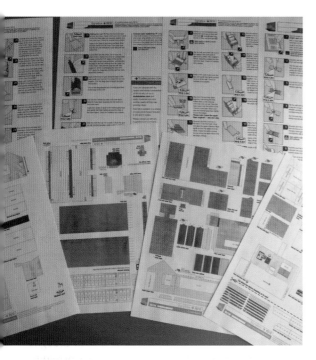

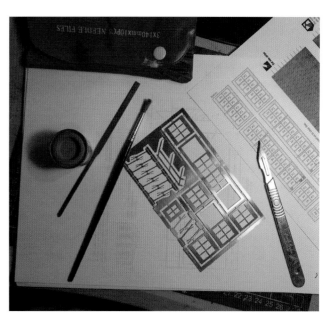

This is a typical Scalescenes download with its easy-to-follow instructions and attractive, clear and nicely executed artwork, all contained in just eight A4 sheets.

Windows are always an important feature on signal boxes. With this kit, as with others in the Scalescenes range, the paper/card version has an alternative in the shape of a small etched fret from Brassmasters. This also includes the handrail and some signal levers. You will need some fine files and a primer.

ABOVE LEFT AND RIGHT: *The brass windows have been brush-primed (Humbrol 1) and given a coat of matt white enamel. It is not easy to get a nice smooth and even-textured finish. On balance, and as wasteful as it may be, a white primer from a spray can would be the better answer.*

later 'three-over-two' style frames – all excellent value for only £2.99 +p&p). Modellers who might be anxious to avoid working with brass will find that the printed glazing from the Prototype range will fit.

The final 'plus' – and it is a big one – is the fact that the kit becomes the property of the purchaser. Reprints of individual sheets or of the full package are entirely free. Mistakes matter much less and, for those with plenty of space, several near-identical kits would not be out of place on the larger layout.

The kit advises two thicknesses of reinforcing card: a small amount of 'light', defined as 200gsm (usually around 0.333mm; a sheet of heavier drawing paper is suitable for this) and 'medium', defined as 1mm thick. This is more difficult to source, so if necessary you can rely on mounting board, which is a tad over-weight but easy to work. Almost half the download is print-only finishing sheets or wrappers.

PREPARATORY WORK: THE ETCHED WINDOWS

It is a matter of personal choice, but it is preferable to get all the preparatory work out of the way before commencing the main assembly. If nothing else, this means that the main task can then proceed without interruption or unnecessary delays.

The optional etched windows will certainly need attention first. As with any brass (or white-metal) components, they must be carefully examined for distortion and flash. The quite flimsy and delicate etch was both accurate and 'true', but there was some evidence of flash or ragged etching – time to reach for the files. These difficulties were perhaps inevitable, considering that the total of forty-five panes equates to no fewer than 190 inside edges to the glazing bars. The solution is simple (if boring): hold the fret steady, with the short side resting firmly on the cutting mat, then use a fine, flat file to work on all the upturned edges of the glazing bars until each one is nicely smooth and shiny. Invert the fret and repeat this top-to-bottom process. Finally, with the fret long side down and using a smaller file, complete the task on the upper and lower edges of each bar. At the end of the exercise, you should have 190 nice shiny edges ready for priming.

A white automotive cellulose primer in an aerosol spray, used in a well-ventilated area in a shed or garage, provides the ideal solution for the next stage. If you have no choice but to work indoors, you will need to source the enamel types of primer that may be brushed on at then bench. All primers need to be allowed to dry thoroughly before applying the white enamel top coat.

ABOVE LEFT AND RIGHT: If you do go down the brush-on route, a little gentle work with some very fine emery paper will improve things.

TOP AND BOTTOM:
With some suitably thick glazing in a place, the judicious use of your scalpel point will help remove any surplus glue and tidy up the corners.

Keep the brush-on primer thin, to avoid any blobs and runners and also to prevent any thickening of the bars. The bars also need to be as thin as possible and, above all, not allowed to bend or distort.

Although this is not a formal review of the various products, there are a number of tips arising from the projects that may prove useful to fellow modellers. In my experience, as a kit-builder dealing with both white-metal and brass-etched components, the results from brush-on primers are at best somewhat dubious. They are difficult to apply, slow to harden and rarely produce an immediately usable finish. Automotive aerosols, on the other hand, deliver almost instantly usable finishes, even to the extent of accepting watercolours when trying to capture the worn and faded hues of wooden farm machinery. The best advice must be, therefore, to invest in a can and be prepared to spend the time in a spray booth (a large cardboard box will do) out in the garage. It will prove to be quicker in the long run.

PREPARATORY WORK: GLAZING AND PAINTING

The next two stages involve painting the frames and glazing bars with matt white and then carefully separating the windows from the fret. Since the kit is a download, you will have to source your own plastiglaze. There are no hard and fast rules for this, but something between 0.05mm and 0.10mm will be about right. To go any thinner risks a wavy appearance to the glazing; going any thicker is overkill and the material will be hard to cut. These two materials, brass and plastic glazing, are never easy to fix; joining them together is even less easy. Reach immediately for the cyano, applying the usual safety caveats and working quickly, dealing with just one window at a time. The throwaway mini tubes from the market or pound shop will suffice for this task. If you are averse to the idea of cyanos, try Deluxe Glue 'n' Glaze.

There are two quite important points to observe, which did not become apparent until further into the assembly process:

1) The actual dimensions of the fret are somewhat out of step with the apertures provided with the kit. The overall lengths of the main front window and sliding side window, which butt on to each other behind the right-hand corner pillar, are a fraction too long to do this. When you add the extra thickness of the glazing sheet, the problem is exacerbated.

2) The second point concerns the relationship between the actual apertures and the inside edges of the main frames. To be visually and architecturally correct, the frames should visible all the way around, emerging from behind the 'timber' structure. However, the front aperture when correctly assembled measures 68.5mm, but the inside edges of the fret are 70mm apart and so are completely hidden.

Sadly, there seems to be no workable solution to these problems. The inner faces of the corner pillars are simply too small to be reduced enough to compensate for incorrect dimensions. Even after taking

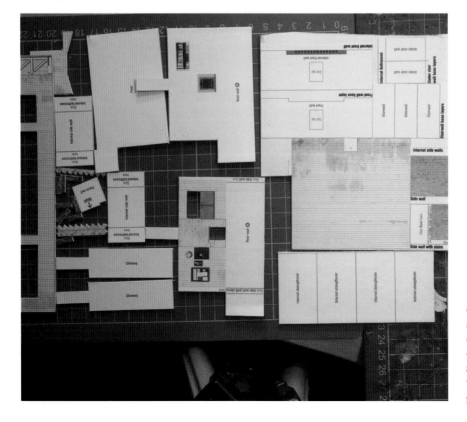

The main components, mounted on thicker card as instructed, can now be separated ready for the eventual build process.

The typical assembly sequence: inner wall, window and frame, outer wall, and finally the print-only brickwork.

them right back to the width of the corner wrappers and trimming the ends of the fret as much as you dare, the result is still far from satisfactory, although it is just about 'passable'. (Having measured the download windows, and allowing for thinner glazing, the original design and instructions will work.)

ASSEMBLING THE KIT

You could do a lot worse than simply following the step-by-step instruction sheets, especially if you have managed to obtain the exact card thickness as advised by the designer, and you have a plentiful supply of replacement blades close at hand. A careful

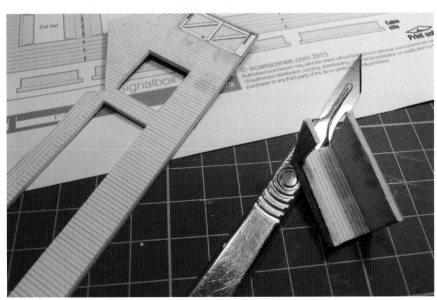

The inside of the upper half/ operating floor together with the small entry porch; a really sharp scalpel is always an essential for accurate and clean cuts.

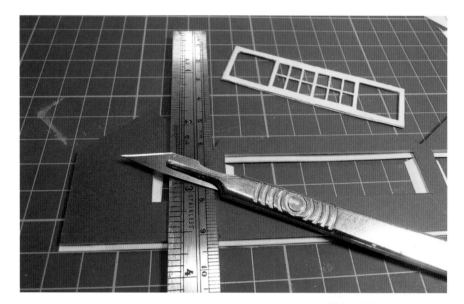

The main window etch has been glazed and is ready to be installed; the open areas are for the sliding sections, which can be fixed fully or partly open or fully closed.

and almost clinical approach to the cutting-out is essential for success. Always cut, or score, along the dead centre of the guides and markings. On small and quite complicated buildings like this, errors of even half a millimetre can cause potential headaches.

My own approach to any kit build is to vary the instructions; a number of key points and issues arose from this particular project, and these are noted below:

- **Preparation:** time, card and blade usage may be saved by cutting out the structural and reinforcing elements first, and then repositioning them on the chosen card in a pattern that minimizes the number of final cuts. It also gives total freedom over the build sequence as all the components are now to hand. Stick and cut them all in one go and put them aside.
- **Sub-assemblies:** experience has shown that it is best practice, with both kits and scratch-builds, to construct as many smaller sub-assemblies as may be practical. These can be worked on from every angle, making it easier to check that each component is well fitted and properly square. Any unforeseen problems are also better sorted out now than on the full assembly. As an added benefit, it means less handling of and less stress on the semi-finished building.

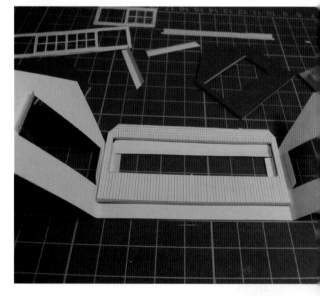

Regular and repeated offering up is one way of avoiding errors and of generally assuring steady progress through the sometimes complicated assembly sequences.

- **Mounting board:** sometimes referred to as 'art board' or 'mount board', this varies in thickness; the version used here (c.01.23mm) was some 25 per cent more than that recommended. This had little adverse effect, except possibly where multiple laminates were concerned, and even then, only the four-up for the chimney required any re-think on

The assembly is coming together quite nicely; even the most basic household adhesives give perfectly acceptable results, at minimal cost. Basic tools are all that are needed for this type of kit.

The sliding windows fit inside and behind the main fixed lights.

ABOVE LEFT AND RIGHT: *The box will have limited interior detail but will not feature the removable roof or rear wall. At this point, the detail can be glued in place.*

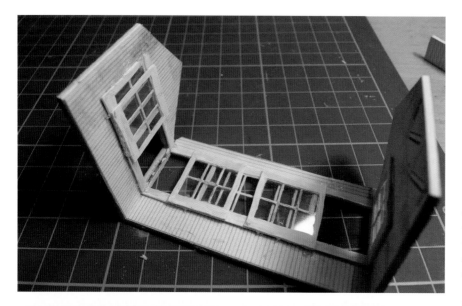

TOP AND BOTTOM: *The three remaining walls for the upper section are designed as a wrap-around. You will need to pay particular attention when forming the corner joints with their brass windows, and some minor adjustments will probably be needed.*

the printed wrapper. On the whole, it produced a neat and robust structure and was, as always, an easy medium with which to work.

- **Overlays/Wrappers:** in general, these were no more difficult than any other pre-printed sheets. They fitted well and without distortion, but they are none too tolerant of gluey fingers, so it is important to be careful. There are some places where the artwork is questionable. For example, on the lobby and the upper floor there are interior and exterior wrappers to be applied to three sides

of a box. No matter how you choose to construct the mounting-board carcass, the interior wrapper will certainly fit; but, because the exterior wrapper is printed to exactly the same length, it cannot possibly fit all the way round the three outer sides.

- **Roof:** there are two issues here. According to the design of the kit, the back wall butt is joined to the two gable ends, forming a 'step' that is two cards thick along the eaves (and four cards thick at the chimney stack). This would not matter if the roof were to sit on top of the wall and then

Fitting the entry porch will need a few minutes' hand pressure to keep it correctly positioned while the glue dries. Use the un-fixed roof template to aid your grip.

The kit is designed to have the roof eaves overhanging the front and back walls, as on the real thing. It is necessary to shave the tops of the walls until they match the angle of the pitch on the gable ends.

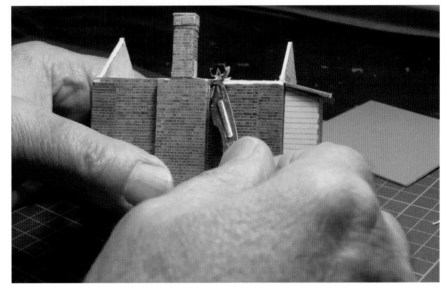

follow the gable ends to the ridge-line. However, it is intended to go the other way, following the gable ends downwards and overhanging the wall by several millimetres. This obviously will not work. Fortunately, the solution is simple: using your scalpel rather like a chisel, carve the top of the wall to match the angle of the gables. While on the subject of the roof, this is designed as another score-and-bend job, complete with its interior sheet, on to which must be glued the tile-spacing guide. Offer up the roof to your freshly carved wall, check it for

alignment and pencil-mark the top of the gables (ridge-line); also make sure that it projects equally at both ends. Cut the roof in two at the ridge, trim either end if necessary, and glue it securely in place. Before you repeat the exercise on the front half, you can finalize and install any interior details and huminiatures.

- **Interior:** in common with most GWR style signal boxes, the operating floor is well lit and an ideal candidate for a fully detailed cabin. However, this particular project was limited to just the free signal levers from the Brassmasters fret. The lever frame is no more than two pieces of mounting board, roughly 2 x ½in. On the edge nearest the windows, sixteen slits were cut to accommodate the pre-painted levers. It is clearly a busy time, since twelve of them have been pulled into the 'off' position. Your choice of colours and assumed roles for them will obviously depend upon the overall role for which the box has been chosen (see also Chapter 2).

- **Access stairs:** these were quite deliberately left until last since they are somewhat accident-prone, especially if the handrail is fitted. The stair treads should be simple thick planks but the overlays on card produce something much heavier. These are more difficult to fit and, in any case, they do not look right. Thin card strips make a good substitute. In respect of the final finish, and as the brass handrails had to be painted, you can give the whole assembly an overall coating in brown watercolour. Enamels or acrylics would work equally well and it

would also help to underline the box's corporate ownership if the appropriate house colours were used.

- **'Corner Caps':** these blue-brick elements should have been pre-glued on to thin card, giving the impression of raised quoins, but a bit of research came up with no examples of boxes with these features. It is true that a great many designs did use blue brick at the corners, but it was always decorative and never in relief. Strictly speaking, they should have been reduced to a one-brick width with alternate courses of three-quarters brick; it is not the easiest of tasks and requires some skilful scalpel work but if your aim is prototype realism then it is worth a try.

CONCLUSIONS

There is little doubt that any downloaded kit will be more demanding than its off-the-shelf counterpart. Downloads are, in principle, only a step or two

ABOVE LEFT AND RIGHT: *Bend-to-fit one-piece roofs rarely deliver the optimum ridge-line. One way of resolving this is to separate the two halves and fit the rear one first, ensuring that it is accurately positioned with the correct overhangs all round. The front portion then overlaps the rear one all along the ridge, to produce a neat joint and a sharp angle.*

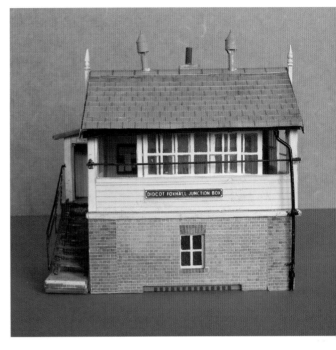

The roof is now complete, bar the final bits of external detailing. The roof edges/eaves have been carefully carved and chamfered to eliminate the otherwise intrusive and unrealistic thick card exposed beneath the slates.

CLOCKWISE FROM ABOVE: *The kit has made up into a nice little GWR/BR(w) signal box, entirely appropriate for any branch-line setting or for use as an intermediate box along a stretch of mainline.*

The TimberTracks signal box looks quite appropriate on the site of Sherborne Tunnel box, where it is given the road to the ex-works (gloss varnished!) Hall.

short of what you might expect to encounter in scratch-building. Because of the number of processes involved, they are not kits to be tackled in a hurry, nor against a tight time-scale. However, if you are modeller who thrives on a challenge and enjoys the opportunity to create something different from the usual high-street options, downloads have much to recommend them.

This Scalescenes signal box took just over a week from start to finish, including the time taken to think out alternative approaches and also to photograph and write up the various aspects.

Following the designer's instructions would doubtless have been quicker, but 'my' finished result is a neat little box (92 x 56mm/23 x 14ft), making it more than suitable for a wide variety of applications. It also offers the opportunity for more detailing inside and outside. By the time it takes its place on 'Wessex Lines', a number of other items will have been added, including gutters, downpipes, finials, a name-board and fire buckets. It is definitely worthy of consideration by a first-time builder, given that they have those pre-requisites mentioned at the outset.

SMART MODELS

This is a relatively new name, but probably familiar to modellers with interests in former LNER territory. Smart have been introducing kits and builder's aids and have over thirty building downloads on offer. They provide examples of a number of different structures, from those designed by the former constituent companies that were amalgamated in the 1923 grouping to the modern boxes built under British Railways, some of which are still working.

This project deals with the rather futuristic-looking box from Low Gates on the former BR North Eastern Region. The building, which is still in operation, dates from 1956 and was significantly modified in the 1970s; both versions are included in the price for the download, which includes free repeat prints if required. This is a large download and you will need a plentiful supply of your best 80gsm paper (or 90 or 100gsm, if you can source any) ready in your printer. There are eight A4 full-colour sheets of components followed by no fewer than sixty numbered A4 full-colour sheets of instructions; needless to say, these will prove costly in terms of ink and paper, so you might prefer to print them as mono A5 files two-up on A4.

The first thing to do is to decide which version you intend to construct: the original, which would be appropriate to the steam era, or the existing style, which would cover the diesel period right through to the present day. Once you have taken that decision, you can safely discard any artwork and instruction sheets that will not be needed. This reduces the amount of paper on your work-bench and simplifies the essential read-through and part-identification process. This process should not be rushed. The building is quite a complex design and is far removed from the traditional 'four walls and a roof' that characterizes most signal boxes. There is only one smallish illustration of the completed structure and you might wish to print an enlarged example to use as a constant reminder.

At first, an online search for further images did not turn up the box. As always, it was the signaller's 'bible' at signalbox.org that came to the rescue. In their 'Photos' section, under BR(NE), there is an indispensable item covering the actual box at Low Gates. There are further images under BR(E) and 'Sleaford South'. It may be enough to study the images and make a few notes/sketches to aid your work, revisiting the site as necessary, but it is advisable to print both these images to a decent size as both information and inspiration. (Please do not resort to illegal downloads and print-outs. The site gives you all the details you need to obtain authorized copies and enables you recognize the hundreds of enthusiast hours that go into creating and maintaining sites such as this.)

PREPARATION

The first and most obvious task is to source the necessary card, adhesives and tools. This kit is no different from any other download and, if anything, it is slightly easier, since there is no requirement for the 2mm heavy card. The instructions advise 200gsm thin and 1mm medium as the cards of choice; 200gsm drawing paper and the thinnest mounting board that was available, which was slightly over-thick, at 1.25mm, worked perfectly well. The usual adhesives – some basic craft PVA, a dispenser of 'Anita's Tacky Glue', UHU and cyano (superglue) – were kept to hand. The tools were equally commonplace, comprising a scalpel and a supply of 10a blades, 6in and 12in steel rulers, a square and pair of small sharp curved scissors.

You can either follow the customary procedure of gluing the whole or part sheets to the appropriate cards before separating the components as required for assembly, or, preferably, separate all the components first then reposition them on their cards and cut them out ready for use. The latter method seems the quicker and easier of the two. One of the key things to remember with this, and indeed all download kits, is that you will find yourself sticking stuck-down paper to stuck-down paper, so it is essential to ensure that every component really is fully and firmly stuck to its backing card.

GETTING STARTED

Dealing with the signal levers was the first challenge – if they went OK, then the rest would surely be

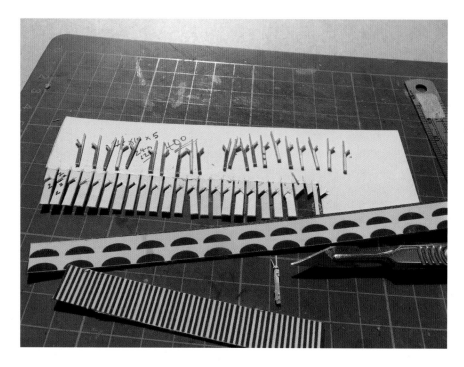

Starting the Smart Models kit in the middle. The signal levers are small and quite fragile so the usual advice applies: take care and use a sharp scalpel. Once they have been cut and laminated they are acceptable, but do not stand up to close comparison with the metal version.

easy? Well, they did go OK, but whether they were worth the effort is debatable. They are, by their very nature, somewhat fiddly items. The first step was to mount the two strips on either side of a piece of thin, good-quality card, ensuring that both strips of twenty-four levers are exactly aligned. This took a bit of head-scratching – the solution was to glue the first strip with their bases along the bottom edge of the card and the first lever touching the left-hand edge. The mirror-image set for the reverse of the card could then be carefully glued down in the same way, but obviously working right to left.

The cutting-out process came next, and the need for a fresh, sharp blade soon became clear. Cutting through a glued multiple laminate of card faced with 80gsm paper demands pressure and accuracy, especially as the components are only 1mm (or less!) in width. 'Make haste slowly' is the best advice to follow. Each lever is a multi-cut operation and separating the whole twenty-four took the best part of two hours and around 400 'cuts'. And the job was not finished then. Remember that these are only slivers of printed paper purporting to represent painted and polished metal. If you want them to be at all realistic, you must treat them in the same way as you would their

white-metal or plastic counterparts, and reach for the enamels or acrylics.

This may be the point at which the question arises of effort versus outcome. Even if the levers are easily seen once installed, they may lack the obvious realism of white-metal castings or plastic mouldings, which are relatively inexpensive alternatives that need only to be painted prior to being installed. The choice is yours…

ASSEMBLING THE KIT

From this point, the procedures are the same as those for the Scalescenes box. Indeed, any and all downloads can be treated the same way, although there are 'best-practice' routines, just as there are for all card or plastic kits.

First, carefully read the instructions and identify the components before separating them from your printed sheets (if that is your chosen method). Since in this particular case there are alternative versions, you should discard anything that is not needed for your chosen build. The next thing is to use your glue-stick to fix all the inner pre-prints and templates to their appropriate card backings and then to remove the various doors and windows. In this case, the window apertures are extremely small square open-

With the main components stuck to their thick card backings, you can begin to separate them and proceed with the assembly.

The smaller the window, the more difficult it becomes to obtain a clean and square cut. There is no easy answer except to practise; use off-cuts and keep at it until you find your own ideal method of keeping the work steady, the ruler properly aligned and the scalpel used to best advantage.

ings. Operations like this are notoriously difficult when working with thickish card (mounting board) – somehow you must combine both pressure and precision to obtain nice vertical cuts that are less than a centimetre long. Only the tip of the blade is available for use and it must be kept upright and held firmly against your straight-edge.

This is the sort of operation that lends itself to the 'batching' of tasks – its very repetitive nature aids concentration and helps to keep your eye in. There is no room for error here as the small flaps for window

openings on the outer pre-print must exactly fit and fold inside these apertures.

The next task is relatively straightforward, at least in principle. In practice, however, it is not without its challenges. Identify the various 'outers' and marry them up with their newly reinforced 'inners'. You will immediately discover that they are mostly over-sized and extend a couple of millimetres beyond the end the walls. This is eventually to help disguise the corners or conceal the edges. The short-term problem is exactly where they should be positioned on the unmarked reverse side of their respective walls. The only conclusion is to ensure that the windows and doors are all perfectly aligned, and then to allow the overhangs to fall where the designer intended.

All the openings and fold-backs were duly cut and offered up and the base of the wall and the pre-print aligned to maintain the horizontal. It is a tricky exercise to slide the artwork back and forth until you achieve the correct position. Nothing can yet be glued down and you are trying to judge the whole thing from both sides at the same time. Patience is essential, especially on that wall with the five small windows.

Windows and Glazing

The area of windows and glazing is a place where there is scope to depart from the kit's instructions and inclusions. Usually, the glazing material supplied is simply too lightweight and, in the case of downloads, the idea of printing on film is even worse. That said, they do work and it is therefore a matter of choice.

Few modellers keep stock of film for the printer, so it will be easier if you can find a suitable sheet of plastiglaze in your stock box, with a thickness of 15thou (0.25mm in modern parlance). For the glazing for the small windows in the walls and doors, it is a simple matter of gluing it with UHU behind the respective apertures. However, when it was offered

it up, it became obvious that it lacked a proper frame. Following the instructions, the outline frames from page 8 were cut out and positioned behind the apertures. A bit of touching up with watercolour disguised any of the white edges, including those on sills and adjacent brickwork.

After this, the fun starts! The main windows on this early version are an extremely complicated design but make a significant contribution to the character of the box. However, from a modelling standpoint, 'complicated' inevitably means delicate, fragile and difficult. One look at the artwork made the problem all too obvious. There are a total of fifty-eight individual panes to be cut out from a single sheet of paper, to leave glazing bars that are 0.01mm thick and about 0.75mm wide. The first move was to find a new blade. The second was to carry out a risk assessment. Even with luck, damage was inevitable, with 232 corners to cut and 464 glazing bars vulnerable to that ultra-sharp blade. If you get away with no more than a dozen damaged, you will have done well.

The next question is how to fix these three flimsy lattices to the chosen glazing sheet – a substance renowned for its resistance to most solvents. The original step-by-step instructions (90 onwards) recommend that the artwork should have been printed on self-adhesive paper and stuck on to the acetate

The ground-floor walls ready to receive their pre-glazed windows. Take care to ensure that they fit nice and square behind the apertures.

before cutting out and removing the fifty-eight individual panes. This is probably easier to describe than to execute. To achieve the precise and perfect cuts, especially into the corners, and to do this without damage to either the fret or to the actual acetate, will take a great deal of skill. However, with repeat downloads free of charge and the fact that you could probably get as many as a dozen sets from single sheets of self-adhesive and acetate, the cost of making mistakes is negligible. The trick is to find a glue that can be brushed on to the back of the fret and then secure it to the plastiglaze. In addition, a priming coat of matt white enamel will add a little extra volume and strength to the delicate tracery.

Which glue worked best? As expected, neither the solvents nor ordinary paper glue achieved anything, and the various PVA-based glues also failed to perform. That left only the cyanos (superglues) and the powerful MekPak, or carbon tetrachloride, which will normally work even on the hardest of plastics. Both of these proved satisfactory, but, given the fact that basic cyanos are very cheap and easy to source, you might choose these. With the benefit of hindsight, Deluxe Glue 'n' Glaze might also have proved to be even more suitable.

The actual fixing with superglue does require a modicum of care as it is a constant battle of speed versus precision. Squeeze a small pool of glue into a spare tin lid, then apply it with your smallest brush to the underside of the fret and work one bay at time. Apply enough glue to get a secure fix, but not too much, or it will seep out and spoil the adjacent panes.

Lever Frame

This small sub-assembly – just 3 × 1cm – will take up a rather disproportionate amount of time for its size. The two rows of half-round prints need to be very firmly fixed to their thin card base. Do not be tempted to use a thicker card or you will make the eventual cutting out even more difficult than it already is. The cutting of semi-circular components with a craft knife or scalpel is never easy and, with items as small as these, a pair of curved-blade scissors are the only answer. Hold the work steady and slowly 'nibble' your way around each one.

The overall appearance of the finished lever frame is somewhat improved when painted with enamels in the same way as its plastic or metal counterparts. This small sub-assembly is now ready to be installed.

The instructions (31–35) give a degree of flexibility on how you use these spacers depending upon the thickness of your card and how many levers you want to install. The actual box has a twenty-one-lever frame and there are enough pieces to mimic this, but you may prefer just to see how many you can accommodate on the base. Pour a small pool of PVA into a spare saucer or tin lid and, holding the item in needle-point tweezers, dip it into the glue and position it as required. It is a slow process but it works and it does give a few valuable seconds to juggle the various bits into their correct positions.

You will need at least a couple of hours to complete the cutting and assembly, at which point you can take a tea break while everything sets. If you add the time spent pre-assembling the levers, then the whole task amounts to a pretty solid evening's work.

The instructions suggest colouring the exposed edges with felt-tip pens. This might be effective, but treating the frame as if it were in plastic or white metal – using enamels and a fine brush – will give a much better result and does not take any longer to achieve. Given the hours invested so far, this extra effort is surely worthwhile. Whether you decide to do it or not, the panel and frame can now be installed.

The Main Assembly

Once you are up to the fifties on the instruction sheets, you are into the building of the operating floor and rear of the box. Follow the instructions carefully and you should avoid any mistakes. You might be forgiven for wondering how it will all turn out, but, as each component and sub-assembly is correctly positioned, the complex structure will gradually take shape. It is wise to offer up the various elements repeatedly to check for fit, alignment and 'squareness'. Any detectable errors can be easily rectified now, but this will prove to be increasingly difficult once things are glued into place. To some extent, small errors are almost inevitable, no matter how experienced a modeller you may be. One component cut to the merest fraction outside the line and the adjacent item cut a whisker inside the line could produce a resultant error of as much as millimetre. That equates to a row of bricks on this particular model. Do not despair – it happens to everyone!

CLOCKWISE FROM TOP LEFT: *The upper (operating) floor will probably represent one of the most challenging aspects of the whole kit. Actual brick walls occupy less than a third of the structure; the remainder is all widows including three corners and six wall fixings.*

The rest of the tasks are quite straightforward, as long as you read and re-read the instructions, even if they are a bit time-consuming. The staircase and treads need particular care in both the cutting and folding operations; do ensure that each sub-assembly is properly square and remains so when you combine them. The actual steps and treads must be identical in every respect if they are to fit correctly. The lower landing seemed to be a poor fit – if you encounter the same problem, simply 'nick out' a millimetre or so to allow the landing to slot back into the upper staircase.

There are a number of other recommendations:

- **Roof supports:** these are tricky little items to cut and fiddly to assemble; each one of the fourteen is a quadruple-laminate (paper/card to card/paper), yet they measure barely a centimetre in length and around two millimetres at the base. Perfection, with all the roof supports identical, is probably unachievable, but do try to ensure that their bases and upper edges are properly aligned. The neatest way of fixing the outer wrappers involves departing from the given advice. Lay the wrapper face down widest end to the left, then place the laminate so that the top side is exactly along the top edge of the wrapper.
- **Roof top:** you may experience a degree of warping or down-turn, especially when the supports are fitted. To correct this, cut a further roof shape from thin card before trimming any overhanging supports and adding the sides. This should not affect the remaining stages.
- **Staircase railings:** the original box clearly has metal railings/handrails, but these are impossible to reproduce via a download. The supplied artwork was difficult to cut with any consistency and a quick offer-up showed them to be 'visually inappropriate' – in other words, they looked awful! The answer lay in using plastic 0.020in micro-rod in the same way as for the safety rails on signals (see the image of Sleaford South referred to earlier). Even so, the very close spacing of the uprights is not achievable within the constraints of the kit. It is a delicate and quite time-consuming task, but worth it if you want

The Low Gates box is a 1950s design and the traditional wooden stairs have been replaced by built-in brick steps. Cutting each step individually is tedious but it is possible to trim off the surplus card and do everything in one operation.

After studying the prototype at signalbox.org. uk, it seemed that abandoning the post-and-rail artwork in the kit was the right decision. The solution had to be as close as possible to metal handrails and that meant searching out suitable plastic micro-rod (0.02in/0.65mm), drilling each step and fixing the pre-cut uprights with small drops of cyano, then using liquid-poly to secure the handrails. It is not 100 per cent accurate but this is not intended as a competition entry!

to capture the character of the Low Gates box. You will need a small pin vice and slightly oversized drill bit, liquid-poly to secure the handrails and drops of superglue to fix the uprights.

CONCLUSIONS

On the positive side this is a low-cost kit of an unusual and distinctive prototype. It would not look out of place on any layout with an NER/LNER setting. The fact that it also offers two versions allows it to fit into the later diesel days and the current scene, as well as the more familiar steam era. The kit itself is imaginatively designed, especially given the complicated structure of the original building; the print quality is well up to standard and the labelling of the components is more than adequate. Like all good kits, it does offer a challenge even to the experienced modeller and, as such, it is not really for anyone in a hurry or

as a first-time venture. Particularly impressive is the fact that the touching-in of any exposed edges took barely a few minutes with the watercolours; indeed, much of that was repairing damages and adjustments.

The sixty or so sheets of instructions may seem somewhat daunting – the designer is clearly keen for the modeller to get the best from his work – but you can save paper if you reduce the size of the text and print them two-up on A4 paper. Some additional and larger images of the actual prototype would be useful or, failing that, similar-sized images of the completed model in both its versions.

The Low Gates kit is at least a three-week task, for a modeller who has a good level of basic skills and experience. Perhaps that is exactly who Smart Models had in mind when they first considered this very interesting addition to the otherwise rather stereotyped range of signal box kits?

LEFT AND OPPOSITE TOP LEFT AND RIGHT: *The rather inadequate windows have now been replaced with these excellent (but costly) retro-fitted versions from York Models. With the roof fitted and a few extras it is now ready to be sited. This modern design would not look out of place in any BR(E) or BR(Ne) location, but it does have quite a large footprint.*

The model was a tricky one to site on 'Wessex Lines'. In the end,
replaced the boiler-house from Winterbourne Dairy!

CHILTERN MODELLING SERVICES

If you are in search of something simple, you could do worse than look at Chiltern Modelling Services (hall-royd-junction.co.uk). Designer John Wallace has successfully amalgamated the vintage approach of the tinplate model era with the twenty-first-century technology of the download kit. Not only that but, for a modest fee, he will supply the download already pre-printed on to quality 335gsm card as a ready-to-cut kit.

The prototype for this particular box is the still-extant former L & NWR example at Hartington on the one-time Ashbourne to Buxton line.

The card kit, which is available in both 4mm and 7mm scale, is ultra-simple, with just two nicely printed sheets. The first contains the entire structure and barge-boards and name-boards; the second provides the roof, access stairs and other details. The instructions are on a single sheet and they also include the necessary guidance for those acquiring the kit as a download.

ASSEMBLING THE KIT

For those who grew up with Hornby clockwork gauge '0', this is rather a nostalgic journey, as many will have owned a 1930s tinplate signal box. This kit will enable you to create something very similar, albeit considerably more realistic and railway-like. The entire job involves only a few hours' work with a sharp scalpel and some appropriate glue – it is just the right sort of project for a tray on the lap and an evening in front of the television.

There is very little advice needed that is not already covered by the instruction sheet. The stair handrails do demand a bit of extra care and patience throughout their construction, and you may wish to score the upper woodwork.

This little model will probably not satisfy the 'Premier Line' purist, but it would certainly fill an otherwise blank space on a layout while you search out a more fitting example. Indeed, if you follow the lead of many of the Bilteezi enthusiasts, then the substitution of proper glazing could well see 'Hartington' as a permanent fixture on an LNWR layout.

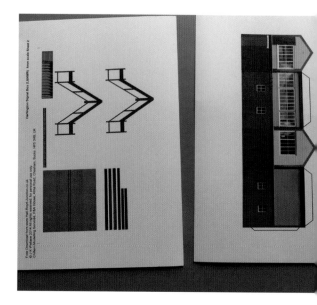

This really is the complete 'kit' for the ultra-simple download from Chiltern Modelling Sevices. It can also be supplied pre-printed on fairly stiff card.

There are a number of points to watch out for:

- **Access steps (1):** these are best dealt with first, when your blade is at its sharpest. It is easier if you 'rough-cut' the artwork to more manageable portions rather than attempting the required precise incisions within the whole sheet. After that, cut out the internal waste areas between the handrails and the bases. This reduces the risk of damage to these ultimately rather fragile components.
- **Access steps (2):** the instructions give you two options: to score and fold or to limit it to a single width with a painted reverse. Frankly, neither method is ideal. On the one hand, the fold must be absolutely accurate or the two halves will not align; on the other hand, the alternative is simply too thin to convince the eye. One solution is to laminate the two complete frets back to back, separate them along the fold line, trim away any too obvious overlaps and then paint the two sections all over with Precision 'Sleeper Grime'.
- **Access steps (3):** there appears to be a slight, although easily corrected, problem with the artwork for the actual treads. As printed they are

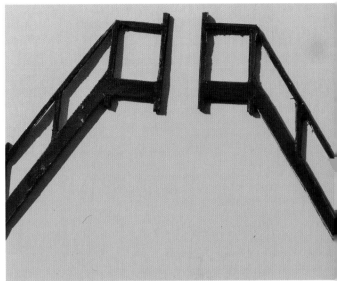

The handrails need care when cutting out and then rely on an accurate 'score-and-bend' exercise.

If you have an aversion to the 'score-and-bend' approach, you can cut each section into two and then carefully laminate them to obtain an optimum result.

too wide and push the right handrail out so far as to finish in the window area rather than against the door framing. Simply trim 3mm off the treads and landing to reduce the overall width of the sub-assembly to around 13mm. Complete the job and set it aside to be fitted last.

• **Main structure:** this score-and-fold exercise is simple, but you do need to make sure that your scoring is sufficiently deep and absolutely vertical. The box seems to have a tendency to adopt a diamond shape with bowed sides. If this occurs, the remedy is simple: cut out two perfect rectangles (of foamboard or mounting card) and make them as 'force-fit' to become the floor and ceiling. Quarter-inch square balsa strips, to brace the corners, proved inadequate. Of course, you could install these from the outset and glue them first to the tabbed wall.

• **Roof:** this was, at best, a tight fit and it was quite tricky to achieve an equal overhang at the eaves. While it is not too visible on the finished model, it does get in the way of an accurate fit for the barge-boards, which should, ideally, be sited beneath and flush with the ends of the tiles and stand clear of the walls. You may have to accept a degree of compro-

ABOVE AND OVERLEAF: *No one could ever assume that this is a typical detailed kit but, printed windows and all, it could still provide a useful stop-gap while deliberating a more permanent replacement.*

mise. It is doubtful that there is any reasonable way of cutting out the elaborate finials, which should, in any case, be mounted on the barge-boards and not integral with them. They are best ignored or replaced by castings.

The end result is quite attractive, but it could be further improved by the addition of a chimney, gutters/down-pipes, fire buckets and other routine details. Matt varnishing is recommended, but best left until the model is finished in order to cover the inevitable and touched-in exposed edges. If you can lightly cover the main windows with masking tape, this will help the final appearance.

Cheap and cheerful, but it still earns its place as a stand-in at Knighton Yard and, as long as you do not look too closely, it is quite acceptable. All in all, it is a nice little kit well suited to the first-time builder.

TRY BEFORE YOU BUY

One of the advantages of the newer technology is that its low overheads enable designers to offer free test models to potential purchasers. These kits may be a bit basic, but they possess all the characteristics and qualities of the full range and will be on your computer in less time than it takes to read about them. The represent a genuine deal that comes with no strings attached.

In order to provide a viable comparison, I downloaded the free trial kit from Smart Models to see how it measured up to the Low Gates example. It gets away to a good start by being based on another box that is still in existence, so it is possible quickly to determine its overall accuracy and print quality. The subject is the former NER box from Carr near Consett, now permanently re-sited at Beamish Open Air Museum (see also Chapter 1). The actual download is four A4 sheets of well-executed artwork

supported by no fewer than twenty-four pages of instructions – ample proof of the quality from this well-respected source.

As a kit, it went together very easily while still adhering to all the recognized assembly techniques. The only fault was that the window artwork did need some touching-in with black ballpoint pen or felt-tip (and this may well have been because of a printing off-day).

For the test, which I have to say it passed with flying colours, I did nothing more than follow the instructions and add the usual thicker plastic glazing. On the layout it stood up well when compared with the whole host of other kits in all the various mediums. It would have provided a perfectly viable basis for the addition of both interior and exterior detailing. Smart Models (and the other designers who offer free trial kits) are to be praised for this welcome initiative to encourage more modellers to get involved in the ever-expanding field of download kits.

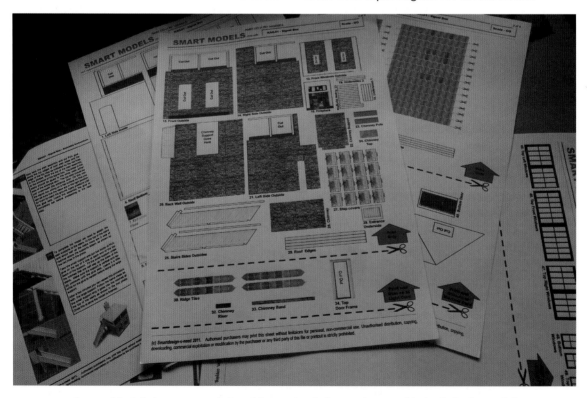

Smart Models have several signal boxes in their catalogue; this is their free trial download of the NER box re-sited at Beamish Open Air Museum – four sheets of well-executed artwork supported by full-colour instructions.

The main kit needs very little attention except that the windows may benefit from some touching in. Any fine ballpoint pen or felt-tip will do the job.

Acting here as Sherborne's 'A' box, the Smart Models kit blends quite well with nearby cottages. It is a sound little piece of design and accuracy, but the addition of some exterior detail and a fully modelled interior would make it even more acceptable to the discerning modeller.

CHAPTER SIX

LOOKING AT LASER-CUT KITS

INTRODUCTION

Laser-cut kits are just beginning to enter the mainstream market and it is impossible accurately to predict their future status. During the last few years, the well-established TimberTracks has been virtually the only name in the game, but larger players such as Metcalfe are now dipping a toe in the water, alongside comparative newcomers such as Smart Models, Osbornes/Arch Laser, 4Track Models and the architectural specialists at York Models. There seems little doubt that, as costs go down and the capability of the technology improves, so more companies will enter the fray. Whether the laser-cut kit will ever replace the universal appeal of the card kit is debatable, since the latter has already more than proved its ability to withstand the challenges posed by plastic, resin and 'stone'.

There will of course always be variations in quality and cost and this is also the case in the world of locomotive and rolling-stock etched-brass kits. The average loco-modeller can obtain quite acceptable results from a kit costing between £100 and £200, but the upper echelons of the hobby demand something more and some are happy to commit four-figure sums in their pursuit of perfection.

There is another facet to these 'etches', which to some extent they share with the products from the plastic and brass manufacturers, namely their role as detailed components for use in scratch-building. They can however go one step further, in that some suppliers are able to produce individually commissioned items and short runs to order. This can be particularly useful when trying to source tricky items such as canopy supports or specialist windows and

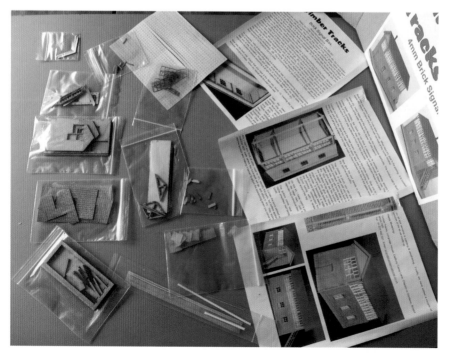

TimberTracks' laser-cut kits come well packaged in a stout carton. The various components, many of which are very small, are separately bagged in plastic wallets, which helps to prevent any losses.

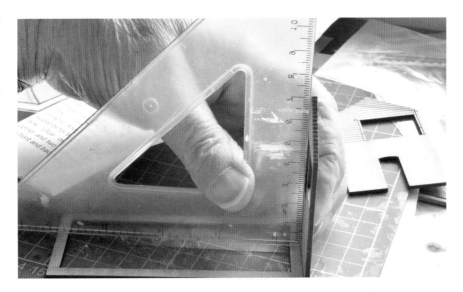

Assembly is perfectly straightforward. The simplest of tools, a steady hand and a bit of patience are all that are needed to ensure those vital right-angles.

it is well worth keeping an eye on the model press and the company websites to keep abreast of developments in this rapidly growing field. Of course, short-run and one-off commissions will not be cheap – you will almost certainly be investing considerably more on your piece of perfect detailing than you spent on the original kit.

TOOLS AND MATERIALS

Laser-cut kits are comparable to card or scratch-building kits and the tools required are similar. In fact, the only additional consideration is that you should heed the manufacturer's advice in respect of adhesives, and have some fine sandpaper to hand in case there are rough or ragged components. As far as the actual finishes are concerned, this will probably be a rather subjective decision. Some of these kits do come pre-coloured, but they may not necessarily blend in with your adjacent structures. It therefore makes sense to have access to exactly the same paint as you have used elsewhere on your railway buildings. It is also likely that the pre-colouring will have been produced by staining rather than painting and, even if the colours are fairly accurate, the resulting appearance and textures will be different.

It seems logical that one weapon in your armoury will be the inevitable scalpel or craft knife, and a plentiful supply of new blades. A small palette knife is a useful aid for applying minimal amounts of glue in exactly the right place.

With regard to the material, you need to be aware that MDF is hard! In its model form it is quite comparable to its thicker DIY origins and requires patience if you need to cut or drill any of the components. Of course, the upside is that the finished kits are sturdy and robust and will last a lifetime without any distortion.

TIMBERTRACKS SIGNAL BOX

How does this TimberTracks product from the upper end of the market compare with the different kits that have been explored? The original prototype is one of the familiar ex-GWR boxes found all over the system. There are many examples still available for study, albeit including several new-builds on the heritage railways. The TimberTracks range includes some thirty or so other kits, most of which have the same GWR origins, notably several station buildings, the excellent Churchward 'loans shed' and the even more magnificent multi-road goods shed that once served Weymouth. Fortunately, while the Weymouth shed will set you back £1,200, the signal box can be yours for a modest £75!

What do you get for your money and how complicated does it look on first encounter? The initial reaction will probably be 'quite a lot' and 'definitely

You can follow your own preferences in the assembly process. The braced carcass, even without a removable rear wall, is rigid and robust; however, it is now easier to access the interior when fitting the windows.

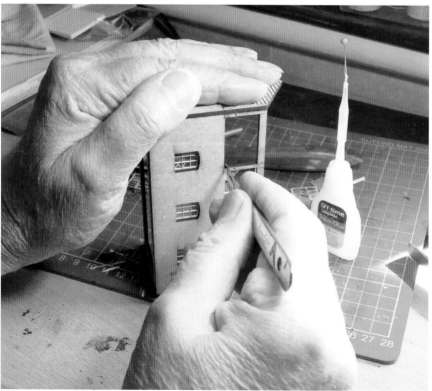

Some trial fitting is as essential on this kit as on any other. A little scraping with a scalpel may be needed to ensure that the windows are a snug fit without being forced into place.

The roof trusses and ridge beam may also need some scraping or sanding. If the square top of the beam does not ultimately follow the pitch of the trusses, the fit of the roof templates will suffer.

manageable'. It is excellently presented and the packaging means that you do not just open the box and find a heap of components, which can be off-putting. Each set of items or sub-assemblies comes in its own small self-seal bag and the kit is supported by a clearly laid-out five-page instruction sheet. Closer examination reveals that even the smallest components are crisply and cleanly cut, with no signs of damage or distortion. Like most plastic kits, it comes as raw material and will eventually require the modeller to apply their own personal paint job. That aside, it is a project that is begging to be built.

PREPARATION

The instructions consist of five large pages of text and images and are written in an easy-to-follow style, giving the impression of a relaxed tutorial rather than taking an over-detailed step-by-step approach. As you might expect with a product of this standard and this level of investment, the makers rightly assume that the prospective modeller is not without a fair degree of experience and expertise. However, they are quick to acknowledge that not

everyone will enjoy a problem-free assembly and have included a 'panic button' phone number for those who run into difficulties.

There are two points to underline: first, they recommend specific glues (Fast Setting Aliphatic Glue/ Product ID TFSG2 – they can supply it direct if you cannot source it locally – and Deluxe Glue 'n' Glaze for attaching the glazing to the frames, or any canopy glue, as used by aviation modellers; second, they recommend that you use a thicker-bladed knife, for example a Stanley knife, for scoring the mortar lines around the corners. A heavier-duty craft knife might also perform well.

ASSEMBLY

Despite the number of parts involved, many of which are extremely small, the actual assembly of the kit is quite straightforward. It certainly does not need a blow-by-blow narrative – the images and the key-point highlights will tell the story. However, in keeping with several of the previous projects, this description will depart from the guiding hand of designer, Brian Lewis, and construct the box with a modelled inte-

Laser-cut components are pretty solid and inflexible items and you will need to use clamps to hold things together while your glues do their job.

rior. The main difference is that the back wall will remain 'removable' and the principle of the slide-in operating floor will be used.

The viability of some other adhesives, which may be more readily available to the average modeller, was also tested.

There are a number of points to consider:

- **Main structure:** some points to consider here; the use of the ring technique is commendable and certainly helps to keep the walls nicely square. Using 'Anita's Tacky Glue' proved quite satisfactory. Assembling the semi-box of front and gable ends in one go enables you to keep a close eye on ensuring that your corner joints are perfectly aligned and your walls are properly upright. Offer up the back wall, without gluing, to check for fit. Remember to fix and glaze the window strip before attaching the 49mm uprights; in order to do their job, they must be level with the top of the window strip. Test-fit the operating floor, to check that it is perfectly horizontal, and then glue it in place. Even without the fixed fourth wall, the structure is now rigid and robust.
- **Main windows:** there can be some potential problems here, so this part of the assembly should

not be rushed. The windows as supplied will work only when modelled as closed and the frames themselves are a fraction tight inside the apertures. You will also need to determine your best sequence for assembly and painting. Having tried the various options, the following order of events seemed to work well:

1) Offer up the main/fixed windows and very carefully sand or scrape the outer ends of the frames and the corresponding sides of the apertures. You want a snug fit, not a forced fit, as the latter would definitely lead to distortion.
2) Place, but do not glue, the above into their respective apertures and then position/check the outer sliding window in the same way.
3) Paint all the windows prior to fitting (with white enamel, white undercoat or acrylic), but avoid getting any on those carefully corrected edges.
4) Check that you have everything the right way round and in the right place, then glue the sliding windows into place at the front of the apertures. Use a very thin cyano with the windows in place and let capillary action do the rest.
5) Repeat for the fixed windows/frames, which must fit tightly up against those already in place.

The finished carcass with its windows glazed and inserted. It is all too easy to leave glue smears during this phase of the assembly.

6) Select all the smaller sections of glazing material and glue them into the frames immediately behind the outer/sliding windows. The larger sections obviously go behind the fixed windows.

7) Use a very small brush to touch up and finalize the paintwork.

- **Other windows and doors:** again, the fit should be snug and never forced or distorted. (NB: departing from the instructions, and not fixing the back wall, proved to be of definite benefit in terms of the ease of access on these tasks.)

- **Roofs:** the spare ring in the kit, as used at the base of the structure, was earmarked for possible use as part of the roof assembly and happily it exactly fitted the purpose. If you are building the version with the removable back wall, offer it up and do any small amounts of sanding necessary to obtain that essential snug fit. It should be glued exactly in line with the tops of the front and back walls; just quickly replace the latter to ensure the ring is horizontal. The four roof trusses now have a bit more support and are easier to fix both square and upright. The rectangular-section ridge piece was very slightly too long, but it was nothing that a few scrapes with the scalpel could not cure.

Once you have glued this item into the slots at top of the trusses, you will notice that its square section is at odds with the triangular profile of the gable ends and assumed profile of those trusses. If it is left unaltered, this will have a marked and adverse effect on the fit of the two roof sections. The simple answer is to let all the glue set firmly and then get to work with the emery paper to restore the correct profile along the whole ridge-line. (By the way, a word of praise for the strips of laser-cut slates: despite being almost miraculously thin, they are still robust and easy to handle. They are quite long, so some carefully ruled horizontal guide-lines may help when sticking them down. A simple glue-stick is more than adequate for this job, with the added bonus that it is easy to apply and dries almost instantly, allowing you to work quickly without risking the soggy mess that can occur with liquid glues.)

Whichever version you are building, the main assembly tasks have now been accomplished and only the stairs and the finishing veneers remain. Keep some cyano/superglue on hand at this stage, as this will be very useful in providing additional and virtually instant reinforcement to any and all joints.

The brick overlays/veneers are now fixed. Make sure you have spread your glue evenly all over the inner surfaces and that the brick courses match at the corners.

With the basic painting under way, it is a good idea to have some suitable prototype images in view. House-colour enamels have been used for the woodwork and watercolour for the bricks; the use of 'engineers' blue' for purely decorative purposes was commonplace on the GWR. It can be picked out with Rowney's Indigo and an ultra-fine brush.

The basic paint job is completed, but there is still considerable work needed to get the tones more accurate. This will probably be a task for the pastels, but it is still too early to put away the watercolours.

Once you are relatively happy with the watercolour stage, you can begin to brush on the various pastel-dust toners. The objective is to get a nice uniform finish, which will hide any obvious brush strokes or uneven densities.

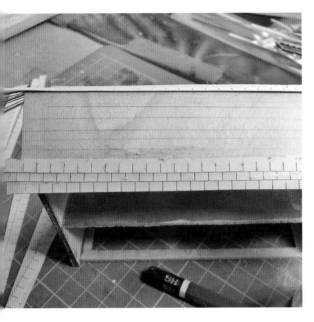 

ABOVE LEFT AND RIGHT: *When fixing the slate strips, use the limit of the laser cuts on the previous strip to get the correct overlap. Some carefully ruled pencil guide-lines will help to keep each strip horizontal. Any glue seepage can be rubbed off with a moistened fingertip, taking care not to damage the surface.*

- **Veneers:** the veneers are superb little items and excellent examples of the Great Western's particular style of brickwork, which featured alternate courses of headers and stretchers. As always, it is as well to do some offering up before you get too busy with the glue. Not only must each veneer fit correctly around the various features and apertures, but they must also have their courses properly aligned at the four corners. As it turned out, the degree of necessary trimming was minimal: the two gable-end walls were an exact fit, the front wall was just over one course too high, and after fixing everything in place just a few millimetres were trimmed from the two main walls. Most of the gluing was done with a version of aliphatic adhesive, brushed thinly on to both the carcass and the veneers, but ordinary PVA should work equally well. Some slight warping led to less than perfect fixing in some places; this was quickly remedied with a few small drops of superglue.
- **Additions:** once the assembly was completed, it seemed as if some elements were missing, particularly the quite pronounced sill beneath the

Staircases are always tricky to assemble and this one is no exception. One solution is to apply the chosen glue to the steps using the tip of a palette knife, then wriggle the treads into place with tweezers.

The various detailing parts were made up almost as per the instructions, but the chimney was altered and narrow strips of ordinary copy paper were used to form the joints on the gutters and down-pipes. These features were 'sweated' in place using liquid-poly and superglue respectively.

Almost there! Note the correct black painted ironwork of the guard rails, the gutters and the top sections of the down-pipes – in line with the prototype references.

main windows and the transom that sits above them. The sills were quickly made from some strip balsa (1.5 x 2.0mm), lightly sanded to give a more realistic appearance. The front and back walls received a combined transom and soffit, this time from a hardwood strip (0.5 x 3.0mm), trimmed to 2.0mm depth for the gable ends. It is only a few minutes' extra thought and extra work and certainly worthwhile.

FINISHING

As always, there are no firm rules applicable to this task, except to remember that it is the 'finish' that the viewer will see and not the craftsman-ship or skilful design that has gone into the actual building. This box was finished with the usual com-bination of watercolours and pastels throughout, with house-colour enamels for the painted wood-work. The job is no more difficult than it would be on any scratch-build or plastic kit. Access to

some coloured images of similar prototypes will help you to get an accurate and handsome model to add to your layout.

A great variety of colour schemes were used by the company's painters. The actual colours may remain the same, but exactly which went where seems a bit open to interpretation. The scheme shown on the box artwork and in the instructions was not convinc-ing – particularly the white-painted guard rail – and a quick delve into the HMRS Colour Register for the GWR confirmed this suspicion. In the end, images of Crowcombe signal box on the West Somerset Railway were used as a guide. Interestingly, the pro-totype paintwork is glossy – as might be expected for exterior finishes – but the model versions are mostly matt. If your model represents one that has had a recent repaint, then you might try finding some close matches from among the general range of glossy enamels. Even the pundits agree that there seem to be no exact and universal values for that elusive 'light and dark stone' scheme.

The finishing touches all come via the SpringSide catalogue (an invaluable source of kits, bits and builder's aids). The distinctive ventilators are a must for any GWR box while the finials are more of an optional extra. The name-boards are from their range of Smith's Accessories; the sheet offers a couple of dozen real locations as well as some hypothetical ones and some ground-frame versions.

The TimberTracks box is ideally suited to a mainline, a busy station or a marshalling yard. It would make a perfect candidate as a replacement at Knighton Yard, although the immediate surroundings would need to change to accommodate the right-handed staircase entry.

OSBORNS/ARCH LASER KIT

This very recent addition to the options available merits inclusion on three counts: its relatively modest price, the unusual choice of subject – the GWR's 'ARP' box – and its absolute simplicity, which made it an ideal project for any newcomer. Like all the railway companies, the Great Western faced many problems during the Second World War. The ever-increasing pressure on freight traffic meant extensive new marshalling yards and other improvements, which obviously entailed many additional signal boxes. That would be taxing enough at the best of times, but the company also faced a nationwide lack of timber and, more importantly, it had to protect its staff and its operations from the unwelcome attentions of the Luftwaffe. The answer lay in the ultra-simple design of the ARP box, with its brick and concrete construction. These were first introduced in 1942/3 and, by the time the last one was built, there were scores to be found all over the system.

(A few years ago, I scratch-built a version for East Ilsley on my exhibition layout. This was inspired by a desire to have something different and was justified by the fact that the DN&SJ Rly constructed several examples further down the line, including one to serve the Naval Air Station at Worthy Down just north of Winchester.)

The Arch Laser model is based on the one at Hinksey South on the mainline between Oxford and Didcot. Building it is completely straightforward and something that can be accomplished within a couple of sessions. There are no awkward roof shapes to deal with and no intricate external staircase. This box really is just that: a box. Despite the low price, the quality of the laser-cutting is extremely good. The character of the box is well captured and everything except the glazing material and safety rail is provided, even a neatly executed name-board. Should you wish to re-site or re-name it, low-cost replacement boards are available from Osborns.

There seem to be no pitfalls to trap the unwary modeller, but there is one point to consider, which probably applies to most of the lower-priced laser-cut kits: creating realistic windows in 4mm scale is never an easy task. All too often they are the Achilles heel of kits in any medium, and they certainly present a challenge for the scratch-builder. Obviously, the problem is exacerbated when it comes to signal boxes. There are so many styles and sizes to contend with and they all have one thing in common: the need to accurately reproduce the quite delicate tracery of frames and glazing bars while maintaining adequate strength and durability. Arch Laser have done a commendable job with these typical GWR 'three-over-two'

Osborne Models offer a growing range of kits, aids and custom-made items via their own exclusive in-house facilities, branded as Arch Laser Cut Kits. The products are cleverly designed to minimize wastage – this signal box is just two frets and is fully cut out.

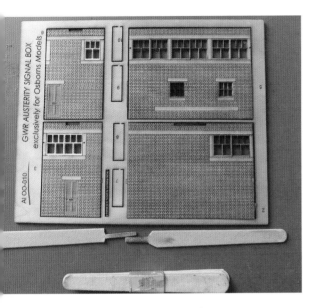

The 'ARP' box is a GWR design and, with minor variations, was widely built across the whole system during the Second World War and up to nationalization. The kit is an ideal choice for a beginner and, with a few modifications, should also meet the needs of the more experienced modeller.

The ARP kit is accurately dimensioned and cleanly cut, but the process inevitably leads to some scorching and roughness. A quick paint job on a couple of windows will reveal the extent of the problem, but it can be speedily rectified with an emery board. Cut a simple tongue in one end of the board to gain access between the glazing bars.

sliding windows, but of course the process of burning through a piece of timber will lead to scorching. As a result, the edges are quite rough and, although this may not be readily apparent to the naked eye, once they have been painted their imperfections become all too visible. This is especially the case if you are accustomed to working with ultra-smooth plastic surfaces.

An hour or so of preparation is therefore recommended, before you reach for the paintbrush. All it takes is some gentle work with specially shaped emery boards, which enable you to reach into areas that would be inaccessible to ordinary sandpaper.

ASSEMBLY

The following advice is intended to supplement the basic instructions. It is in no way essential to follow it, in order to obtain a highly satisfactory end product, but it may prove helpful:

- **Glazing:** use a reasonably thick sheet and fix it to all the windows before assembling the walls. Try to leave at least 1mm clear of the corners to avoid the glazing impeding the neatly chamfered joints.

- **Floor supports:** these are also best fitted ahead of the main assembly. To be strictly accurate they should be fixed from the window down rather than from the base up. This is because the floor on the ARP boxes was much higher than on all the other types, at barely 9in (instead of 30in elsewhere) below the window sills. On the model this means fixing them 5mm below the window line. This is a 'must' if you intend to model the interior.

- **Assembling the walls:** the chamfered joints are very accurately cut and they may prove tricky to align using the building jig. It might be preferable to use the more traditional method of combining each pair by hand and eye, with the aid of a simple set-square. The base can then be fixed to the first pair as per the instructions, using a generous fillet of balsa cement to the top of the joint while holding the whole sub-assembly firmly in place, to ensure

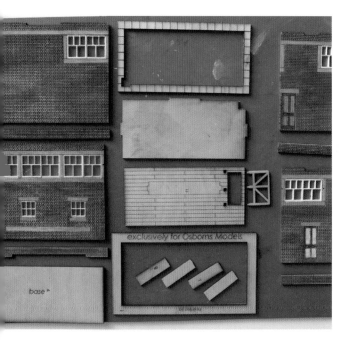

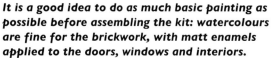

It is a good idea to do as much basic painting as possible before assembling the kit: watercolours are fine for the brickwork, with matt enamels applied to the doors, windows and interiors.

The operating floors were set much higher than normal on these ARP boxes. This can be replicated by simply fixing the mounting blocks higher up the walls, taking your measurements relative to the window sills.

The kit includes templates to help keep the walls square during assembly. Join them up as two sub-assemblies off site, using a set square, and then use the templates for the final joins. Any adjustments can be made before the adhesive sets.

ABOVE LEFT AND RIGHT: *Close to completion: it takes barely a few hours to reach this stage. If the detailed interior is not required, the job is virtually finished, even down to the 'South Hinksey Signal Box' name-board. Alternative names can be speedily cut as bespoke orders.*

ABOVE LEFT AND RIGHT: *The finished box is ready to be sited, after fitting a down-pipe at the back to drain the roof. (There is no conclusive evidence about gutters, down-pipes or other external features, which probably varied from box to box.) The black safety rail is in its correct position halfway up the lower window panes.*

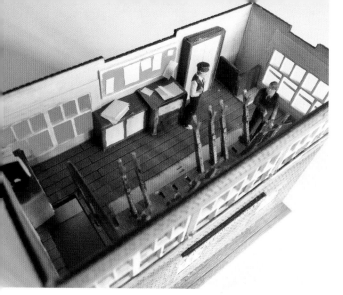

ABOVE LEFT AND RIGHT: *The roof is easily lifted off to reveal an interior that was quickly knocked up from scrap card and paper. Given the high floor and multiple windows (which have some very fine-cut bars), this is one occasion where a degree of detailing is almost essential.*

South Oxford has been swapped for South Devon but the ARP box does not look at all out of place.

the optimum fit. The second pair then follow, with particular attention given to the two corner joints.

FOR THE PURIST

While there were many such ARP boxes constructed during the war, it will come as no surprise to learn that images of them are few and far between. Many were located in areas not frequented by photographers, either due to war-time restrictions or because they were inaccessible, or perhaps they were just uninteresting to the post-war cameramen. However, a trawl through my own library and the internet has

turned up a few points that might be helpful to modellers in search of greater accuracy.

The brickwork obviously varied from location to location and Hinksey South used a very orange-toned brick, which still tended to look rather 'raw' even as late as the 1950s. All the images show a single access door at the left-hand end, making the second door in the kit incorrect. (That said, the only images of Hinksey South show no doors at all so maybe it was in the rear of the building?) There seems to be no reference showing a box with a decorative plinth, so this could or should be omitted – remembering to

The ARP box has now taken up permanent residence on 'Wessex Lines' at Stoneycombe. Its proximity to the very active quarry on the famous Dainton Bank saw the GWR siting a similar box, not to protect against the Luftwaffe but against rock falls caused by over-enthusiastic blasting!

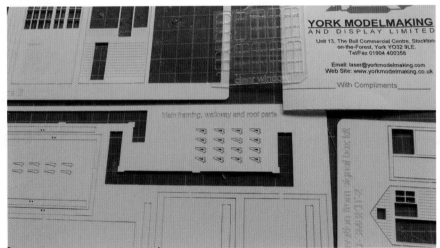

Some of the finely cut items for the Midland signal box produced by York Models; their website is a must for anyone scratch-building, detailing or looking for an upmarket kit.

cut a new exit slot for the wires and rodding. Finally, the question of the safety rails is a bit contentious, as the floors were higher than usual, thus placing the window sills at barely knee height. This would seem to suggest that the rails should, if placed at the appropriate safety level (say 42in, or just over 1m, above the floor), make the holes in the kit appear correct. However, the photos of South Hinksey and all the other boxes clearly show the rails positioned halfway up the main window panes, in the traditional manner. The choice is yours!

CONCLUSIONS

Laser-cut kits should hold no terrors, even for the novice builder. The tools and skills required are no different than for any other kit and, while previous experience is obviously an advantage, a modicum of care and a degree of patience are all that is really needed. It is true that some of the ranges are quite expensive and might well cost more than the average modeller would wish to invest. However, for the modeller who is in pursuit of individuality, accuracy and an enjoyable modelling experience – and wishes to steer clear of scratch-building – these kits could prove to be the perfect answer.

CHAPTER SEVEN

SCRATCH-BUILDING YOUR OWN SIGNAL BOX

Over the years, a number of myths and legends have arisen surrounding the art of scratch-building. It has acquired a status in the model world that is actually way in excess of its rightful position. True, there are a number of 'premier-league' modellers, whose work really is on different plane – whether they use card, plastic or metal, or whether they specialize in locos, rolling stock or structures, their results mark them out as the true professionals within the hobby – but there are also hundreds of other players who are regular and highly competent performers. These people get involved for their own pleasure and satisfaction, and for the enjoyment of others who see their efforts at exhibitions or in the model press. Good scratch-building is simply an extension of the skills learned through kit construction, allied to a strong inclination to build either something different or a specific subject, as well as a willingness to master a few basics about drawing and measurement. Effectively, scratch-building is no more complicated than constructing a 'kit' that you yourself have designed.

If this is your first attempt at scratch-building, a signal box is the ideal subject. It is, after all, just a box. It is also, as a general rule, a relatively small structure, constructed of the simplest materials and with minimal fancy decorative embellishments. Signal boxes boast only two roof types – hipped or ridge – and even their chimneys are often no more than a stovepipe. There are still some challenges but you should be able to end up with some creditable reproductions of real-life (and still working) prototypes.

Tunnel Junction on 'Wessex Lines', a scratch-built version of the real thing that once occupied a similar location at Salisbury. Based on just three mono images, it may not be absolutely accurate.

STUDYING THE PROTOTYPE

There are a few basic rules regarding the real-life signal box; some have already been identified, but they will be covered again here, in order to keep all the information in one place:

- **Prototype materials:** signal boxes were often built of the same materials as the other structures in the station area or on that particular stretch of line; in which case, it would be either a local brick or the type consistently used in vast quantities by the operating company. Where the stations were built of local stone, the box might feature a stone base with a wood-planked upper floor. A third, and fairly common, version could be virtually all timber but constructed on a brick or stone plinth.
- **Calculating dimensions:** if your intention is to model a box that includes brickwork, the dimensions to remember are that mass-produced bricks measure (in inches) 9 long x 4 wide x 3 deep, separated by ½-in mortar courses. This should help you calculate the size of the 'wall'. Count the number of bricks laid lengthways ('headers') and multiply by 9in or by 3mm to get an immediate answer for

the length in '00' scale; then, for greater accuracy, add in a ½-in allowance for the number of mortar courses. Most brickwork will include a number of visible half-bricks or bricks laid end-on. These will be near certainties on corners and around door or window apertures; allow 1.1mm for these.
- Height is calculated in the same way, but here the sum is 'number x 3in/1mm' plus mortar courses. When it comes to reproducing this, unless you are very skilled with a paintbrush, it is best to use a suitable proprietary brick paper.
- **Timber-built:** signal boxes constructed wholly from planked cladding on a wood frame were quite common on most regions. The use of timber for just the upper (operating) floor was perhaps even more plentiful. There is no general rule on whether the planks should always be laid vertically or horizontally, nor is there any consistency in respect of their sizes. Most seem to be the tongue-and-groove type, usually 8ft long and from 6in to 8in wide. That said, if you want a version with horizontal 'shiplap' overlapping planks, you will be sure to find an example somewhere out there.
- **Slate roofs:** the moulded roofs on plastic kits are never very satisfactory, and scratch-building offers

Dainton Summit signal box, with its fully detailed interior, occupies a rather different location to its Devon prototype. It is totally reliant on research from the steam albums.

the opportunity to improve on them. The majority of signal boxes (if not all) had slate roofs and most of these would use the typical Welsh slate that can be seen all over the country. The size of these slates could vary significantly to suit the particular roof and, doubtless, to meet the builder's demand for cost and convenience. Whatever size was used, the one thing they had in common was their thickness. Slates are generally less than ½in thick (at the most), even at their centre, and are chamfered almost to a cutting edge at the end. At normal viewing distance, this makes the 'steps' between the rows and the gaps between each slate virtually imperceptible. Even a full ¼in in our 4mm scale is still only 0.08mm, which is less than the thickness of cheap copy paper.

Common slate names and sizes include the following:

- Single 10 x 5in;
- Double 12 x 6in (4 x 2mm);
- Countess 20 x 10in;
- Duchess 24 x 12in (8 x 4mm);
- Empress 26 x 16in.

MATERIALS, GLUES AND TOOLS

- **Card and paper:** although plastic sheet may be used in scratch-building, card and paper are generally easier for the newer modeller to source and to work with; they are also less toxic, so the desk in the corner of the lounge or the tray on the kitchen table remains an acceptable workplace. The availability and variety of usable paper and card has never been better. Decent-quality materials are no longer confined to art shops and hobby or craft stores; most pound shops and discounters have plenty on offer.
- **Mounting board:** the list of all the sources and types of card and paper that the scratch-builder can put to good use is a long one. Fortunately, because the amounts needed are relatively small, it is possible to keep a supply of almost everything close to hand. A simple wallet-style office folder will hold enough to complete dozens of projects. Top of the list of must-haves is probably mounting board, sometimes called art board. This can be used to reinforce thinner card, as a shell or carcass, or for whole buildings. It normally comes as an A1

Regardless of the starting point, the ultimate goal of scratch-building is a layout almost devoid of kits or ready-to-site models. This version of King Charles Cottage and smithy was inspired by Roye England's exquisite model at Pendon Museum; the group also includes my childhood home in Ivy Cottage on the left!

sheet, but A3 can be found; heavier kitchen scissors will swiftly hack it into more manageable sections. Beyond that, you can stockpile anything and everything from cigarette papers to cereal packets or the backs of A4 pads.

- **Wood, plastic strip and micro-rod:** other useful materials include lengths of wood, both balsa and hardwood, in a variety of strips and shapes. Some plastic strip and micro-rod can make a valuable contribution for smaller and more delicate items that are difficult to fabricate from anything else.

- **Glues:** adhesives are easy to source and to use. Specialist glues are not necessary; they are invariably quite costly and you can achieve the same results for a few pence spent on the high street or local market. My own work-bench boasts nothing more fanciful than a large pot of PVA, tubes of clear glue, glue-sticks and glue-pens, balsa cement, liquid and 'poly' and some cheap superglue for smaller items. Some Plasticine or Blu-tack is also useful for temporary holding.

- **Tool kit:** the tools you choose need be no more complicated than the other elements. First and foremost, always work under a good light and, if you are a glasses wearer, pick the pair best suited to the task. Take great care not to strain your eyes, as they are the modeller's most valuable and irreplaceable tool. You will need good cutting instruments; a scalpel and a 10a blade do most jobs, but a heavier craft knife is also useful, if only for the thicker card. A selection of scissors is a worthwhile investment as are various tweezers; try the tool stall in your nearest market for the surgical type. Palette knives make excellent spreaders for PVA or paper glue and can be used to smooth out and firm down the various finishing sheets. Lastly, various sizes of bulldog clips will hold smaller laminates together while the adhesive cures; for larger sections a pile of old magazines will make a good weight.

- **Builder's aids:** there is a whole range of 'builder's aids' available to serve the scratch-builder or kit-customizer. It is so wide-ranging that it is difficult to classify them all under particular headings. Is a brass or white-metal chimney pot a 'finish'

alongside brick or tile papers, or an 'accessory' like a dustbin or fire bucket? Is it an essential or an optional extra replacing a simple tube of rolled paper? If it is something that you can buy and install more quickly and to a higher standard than you can fabricate, it is definitely an 'aid' to your efforts as a builder. The more projects you undertake, the more use you will find for these items, be they in the form of a mini-kit, an off-the-shelf accessory pack or a few one-off castings. Shop around online or browse the adverts and reviews; check what your local dealer has in store and visit the specialist stands at exhibitions. You simply cannot have too much in your bits box.

LOCATING A SUITABLE SUBJECT

With so many kits readily available, not to mention the further opportunities to 'customize' these into many different variations, you might think that there is little need to even consider scratch-building. However, this route is not always taken out of necessity; it is an enjoyable and rewarding part of the hobby and it does not matter if your layout never leaves home or is never seen by anyone other than yourself. There is great satisfaction in knowing that a particular model is entirely your own work. Without your enterprise, effort and skills it simply would not exist and there is no other model exactly like it in the world. If you have never scratch-built before, take this opportunity to have a go and create something that will be unique to your railway.

A signal box is an ideal place to start since its very nature lends itself to this technique. It is a relatively small and compact structure; it is robust and will need little in the way of additional bracing; it oozes character and sense of purpose; there is a vast array of prototype examples, both in the archives and on the many tourist railways; and there is wide selection of readily available modeller's aids for the tricky bits and the subsequent detailing. The projects detailed here will reproduce three boxes, all of which are very much in daily use on two of the best-known tourist lines, or heritage railways. They all make use of field

A simple exercise in DIY modelling – a wartime GWR box based on several examples that were built in 1943 as part of the D-Day upgrading of DN&SJunc.Rly. For the record, train number '320' refers to the down Devonian and Castle 4016 South Wales Borderers has the up working; 4016 was a long-term resident at Newton Abbott. This ancient Dublo model is still in service after fifty years.

research, but this could and should always be further supported by both archive and contemporary images and information.

The most southerly example is the quite recently commissioned version of an ex-LSWR box at Corfe Castle on the Swanage Railway. The other two can both be found on the West Somerset Railway; the first is the standard ex-GWR box at Blue Anchor and the second is the very last surviving working box built by contractors Saxby & Farmer to a design by the original Bristol & Exeter Railway at Williton. All three are relatively small structures, which makes them ideal subjects for any branch line or for installation as an intermediate box or at a wayside station on the mainline; as an added 'plus', they also span all the steam-era decades, from pre-grouping to preservation. Together they offer an interesting contrast in styles and also in the materials used in their construction.

They are also all platform-mounted boxes, which makes them much easier to access and to measure for the interior details that could be included. This is a useful point to remember if you intend to embark on a similar exercise of your own. If you can find a suitable subject, a platform-mounted box cuts out any need for prior approval, lineside pass and pos-

sible escort. An on-the-day request via the station staff to the duty signalman will invariably be met with kindness and co-operation. A few coins in the collecting box will often smooth the way!

BEFORE YOU START – BASIC ANALYSIS

As is the case with learning any technique or new skill, there are a few basics to understand first. Where scratch-building is concerned, these will apply no matter what structure you are considering as your project. The first of these is so basic that it hardly bears restating: make sure your chosen building is one that is truly 'fit for purpose'. All the following aspects have equal importance: is it the right one for the role for which it is intended on the layout? Will it fit the location and footprint you have assigned? Is it right in terms of period and geography? Is there a good resource for research material? Can it be easily accessed on a field visit for photography and measurements? Are there 'modeller's aids' available should they be needed? Finally, do you have (or think you can master) the required skills to build it in the medium of your choice?

A fraction of the range of builder's aids from York Models. Some of the more difficult aspects of construction can often be resolved by the judicious use of such items, which are offered, either off the shelf or custom-made, by many suppliers.

This may seem a little pedantic, but if this is your first venture and you come up with some genuine negatives, perhaps it is best to have another think. As you grow more experienced, these points will all become second nature. It is a shame to take the time and trouble to design and construct a credible model, for example, only to find that it is a few irritating centimetres too large to fit the site.

In an effort to include as much variety and interest as possible, each project will feature slightly different construction techniques. They are all fully inter-changeable and can be 'mixed and matched' to best suit your chosen subject. They should also enable you to make the best and most agreeable use of your time and talents. Try not to lose sight of the fact that this is a hobby and should always be a source of enjoyment. If it becomes too stressful and unsatisfying, you might want to think about selling the lot and taking up golf!

The main variations will be in the area of the carcass and the bracing or reinforcing materials. One project will feature mounting board, another will have a lightweight exterior supported by foam-board, while the third venture will make use of a balsa-wood shell.

Blue Anchor signal box on the West Somerset Railway. Where possible, do a field visit and take as many photographs and measurements as you can. Always seek permission, do not trespass and try not to get in the way.

Note: the Blue Anchor will be the first of three scratch-build projects. Even if you intend to model one of the other boxes, do read through the Blue Anchor section first and be prepared to refer back to it. It contains most of the 'all-you-need-to-know' information and the other sections will omit much of the detail common to all the projects. If you are using the data that is shown, it is best to use it only as a guide and always work with your own results.

THE BLUE ANCHOR SIGNAL BOX

For this first project, much of the basic analytical work has been done for you. The box is intended to control a typical small branch-line station some-where on the GWR/BR(W) and in particular it will look after a level-crossing on the approach. It will be sited at the end of a platform and research shows that it will just fit in the available space. That is a positive answer to one of your basic questions. This standard-style GWR box, built in 1904, was common across the whole system and lasted well into the diesel era. There are scores of images of Blue Anchor and of identical boxes, and access is actually on the station, so a field survey is a practical proposition – another positive answer. There are certainly acces-sory packs for the windows, ventilators and other items, together with kits for the interior details – another positive.

Do you have the skills to carry it out, though? The answer is 'yes', as it will be constructed from card and suitable brick papers. If plastic sheets were to be used for the first time, that answer might well have been 'no', as the subject is too complicated and requires too much precision. The solution is to find a simpler structure (which is difficult) or change the medium (which is easy!).

FIELD RESEARCH

Once the decision-making phase has been satisfac-torily completed, you can plan your field visit. The objectives will be exactly the same as for all such visits: to take as many photographs as are necessary to be able accurately to draw the four elevations (the sides, in everyday speak), the more prominent features and any specifics.

The external measurements are obviously critical and, if you have a companion with you, a 25-metre tape is the best answer. If you are on your own, you will need to have a simple measuring-stick to use in conjunction with your photos. This invaluable piece of equipment is easy to make. It is just a piece of strip-wood four or five feet long with each alternate

The starting point for any scratch-building exercise: the measurements and blown-up photographs are extrapolated into a detailed working drawing that will be the basis for final artwork.

foot painted black or white. This stands out well on the images and, judiciously placed, should enable you to calculate the various dimensions on your return.

For this kind of project, the interior also needs to be recorded. Once again, it is best to take as many photographs as you can without overstaying your welcome and getting in the way – do study the time-table and enter the box only during the lengthier intervals between the services. If you subsequently decide to just 'fudge' the interior, you can simply discard some of your work. You might also wish to ask for permission to linger and record the closing of the crossing-gates ahead of the next up-working.

DRAWING THE 'KIT'

The next step is to transfer your images on to your computer and print them off. The quantity and size are up to you, but it would be sensible to print the elevations to at least A4 in full colour and with virtually no background detail. These will be large enough for you to use the measuring-stick to calculate all the key dimensions. (There is no need to print on photo paper; 80gsm copier paper is more than adequate.) These can be recorded in feet and inches and then

transferred on to the drawing as 4mm/1ft markings, or you can skip the Imperial measurements and draw straight from the photograph, each black or white division on the stick now becoming 4mm on the drawing. The useful rule of thumb on brick-built structures is to count the actual bricks and assume that they are 3mm long (9in) and 1mm deep (3in); half-bricks are actually 4in wide and are not true halves, so you need to a bit of juggling for these and for the ½-in mortar courses. By mixing the two techniques, your final artwork will rarely be more than plus or minus one per cent adrift – it is very unlikely that anyone will be able to spot that on your finished model!

The end result of these deliberations revealed a box measuring 20ft x 11ft 9in (80 x 47mm), plus the porch, which increases the length by a further 2ft 9in (11mm).

Mounting board has all the properties necessary for a kit of this size. It is inexpensive and has a good surface texture, it cuts relatively easily but is sufficiently stiff to minimize the need for additional bracing. A project of these dimensions will require only a smallish work-piece. The surfaces will be

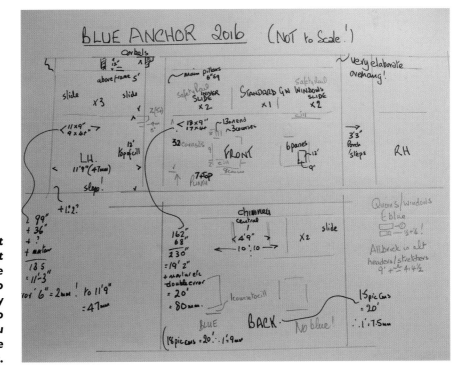

In order to get things right, not just in scale with the prototype but also to incorporate any minor changes to fit your layout, you will need to do some maths.

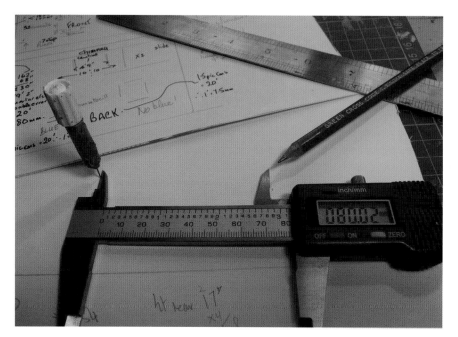

Transferring your calculations to your work-piece is a straightforward task, as long as you have a sharp pencil; a digital Vernier scale is a huge help too, as is a simple needle, suitably protected.

covered eventually in the correct style of brick paper, which means you could use the grey side as the outer walls and leave the white, which is better suited to detail, for the interior. Alternatively, you could have it white side out, and use it for calculations or instructions.

Before you start drawing lines, it is probably a good idea to quickly sketch your best options for the final design.

Although the Blue Anchor box can be described as being platform-mounted, it is a bit more complicated than usual. The field visit and the resulting photographs will reveal that it is actually set into the platform rather than sitting on it and that there is a very noticeable change in the ground levels front to back. This of course means that the kit needs to be drawn upwards from real ground level. The rear and the road-side ends will both be fully finished, the front will be partially finished to cope with the platform ramp, and only the station end and entry steps will be done to platform level. In essence, it is a ground-level box set into a recessed platform. The added benefit, of this is that the finished box may be easily modified and sited at track level in an alternative setting, without the need to alter any of the key dimensions.

(In view of the modelled location, this is one instance where the kit could have been drawn without the customary foundations. Most of the join at baseboard level will be hidden from view and a foundation strip would merely make life more complicated when merging the box with the platform. However, since this is a demonstration exercise, best practice has been followed.)

In drawing the four elevations, the first line is the continuous baseline, which should extend beyond the combined lengths of the walls. Before plotting the upright corners, you need to decide whether you are going to assemble the structure by score-and-bend or by the easier butt-joint method. For the former, the corners should be marked exactly as per calculations. For the latter method, you need to adjust (shorten) the two gable ends by the exact thickness of two layers of mounting board. These will subsequently fit between the front and rear walls, thus restoring the correct dimensions. Plot the height of the walls, making due allowance for the overhanging roof, then draw the eaves line to complete the very basic box. (See the diagrams for these aspects in Appendix I.)

TACKLING THE ROOF

Before cutting anything, plot and draw all the window and door apertures. These will require considerable care if you are to get them exactly right in terms of their individual dimensions and their relative positions. This is also a good time to calculate and draw the roof template. The roof has little to do with the overall robustness of the model and it needs to be shaped in very precise angles in two aspects. You can discount the thickness and strength of the mounting board and select a lighter-weight card – the back of an A4 pad will be adequate for this job.

The hipped-roof design on the Great Western signal boxes is undoubtedly very attractive to look at, but can be a real pain to model. This is particularly the case on the smaller boxes, since they often have very little in the way of a ridge-line. There are two ways of tackling the problem. The first, and on balance the better of the two, is to draw and make the roof from one single piece of artwork. This has long been the method favoured by the kit designers and, unsurprisingly, works equally well for the scratch-builder. The other option is to produce the artwork as four separate pieces, in two pairs – one identical pair for the front and rear, and the second matching pair for two ends. In both cases, accuracy is vital. Every measurement must be precise and every angle must be both correct and identical to its fellows.

Unfortunately, the one measurement that would prove to be invaluable is the very one that is impossible to obtain – namely the actual vertical height of the roof. There is little alternative but to rely on the measurements that can be interpreted from your photographs and then test these with some scale drawings and perhaps even some paper mock-ups. The construction method is irrelevant, as the resulting dimensions are obviously common to both.

The one measurement that can be derived fairly easily from the photos is the length of the roof at the eaves:

1) Start with a horizontal line that is similar to the one with which you began the walls;
2) mark out the length of the front of the eaves (working from left to right), then draw a line perpendicular to this of the correct length of the right-hand eaves;
3) using your set-square to get another 90-degree angle, draw the rear eaves exactly parallel to and of the same length as those at the front;
4) finally, turn this eaves line through another right-angle and draw in the left-hand eaves.

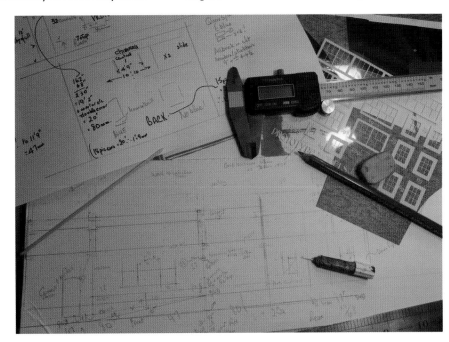

Accurate glazing is vital with signal boxes and is immediately characteristic of the railway being modelled. This is typically an area where builder's aids come into their own.

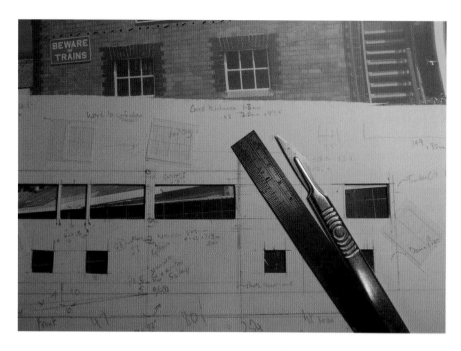

Cut all the apertures for the windows and doors while the work-piece is still intact; this is also the time to decide how you intend to form the corners and whether you will install floors, ceilings and a detailed interior. Always remember the old maxim: 'Measure twice and cut once'!

If you have plotted it all correctly, you should have arrived back at the point from which you started – namely the extreme left-hand end of the front eaves. If you are anywhere else, then an angle or measurement must be wrong, so you will have to find and correct the error before going to the next stage, which is the tricky bit.

It is probably pretty obvious that simply drawing in the four diagonals leading from the corners to the ridge-line will not work. The drawing needs to be opened out to create the extra space required by the height of the four segments of the roof. Using the dividers or Vernier scale on the elevations suggests that the ridge-line from the eaves is equal to one-fifth of the full height of the walls. (Using your own measurements, that should be one-fifth of 72mm, or approximately 15mm.) This may not give a precisely exact dimension and there is still some way to go. The only way to prove your calculation is to make a test drawing on piece of copy paper and actually cut and fold it into shape. (If you happen to have the Prototype GW model to hand, you can always check your findings against their acknowledged accuracy.) It is then a question of visual judgement: if it looks right against your photographs, you can go ahead and transfer the drawing on to your artwork. If it is not quite right, it may look too high and too steeply pitched or too low and too flat.

MODELLER'S LICENCE

The Blue Anchor box is an example where something not strictly necessary can be included and put to good use. It is a known fact that most real-life signal boxes did not have ceilings, at least in the accepted sense. The majority, and Blue Anchor is among that number, simply had their boarded under-roof and trusses painted white. There is no actual need to model a ceiling, but why not do so? It will be most useful in this planning and construction phase and it will serve as a firm base on which to build the roof. It would also make it more robust should you opt to construct it in a removable form. Mounting board is the best material. Simply draw and cut out a small rectangle to the exact outer dimensions of the walls, plus the very distinctive corbels; in practice it will sit on these, with the slate roof itself overhanging the eaves.

Having cut your rectangle to approximately 90 x 60mm, you could use it white side down to help illuminate the interior. On the upper surface, draw a line exactly parallel to the longer sides right across the centre of the piece; this will obviously bisect the

When using pre-printed sheets, it is worth checking to see if these can also be fixed before the walls are separated, or deeply grooved for a score-and-bend version.

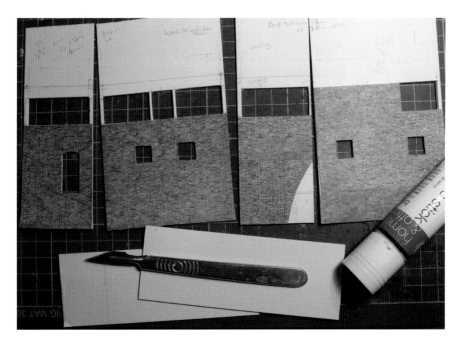

shorter sides and be located 30mm from their corners. You now need to find its dead centre lengthwise – it should be 45mm from each end. The calculated length of the ridge-line is 28mm, so you can plot two marks at 14mm from that central point. (Actually doing all this is probably quicker than trying to describe it.) Note that you can remove the central area of the base in order to give easy access to the underside of the roof sections when gluing and positioning.

Cut two shallow triangles from your board. The base of these will be the full width of the ceiling and their height where they cross the centre-line/ridge-line must be your previously calculated 10mm. These can then be glued squarely and vertically across the ceiling, exactly on to the two marks that indicate the ends of the eventual ridge.

Now you need to test your theories with a mock-up. Use thick paper or thin card cut as a rectangle a few centimetres larger all round than your ceiling. Fold it in half with a crease that is nice and clean, and dead straight, then, using the crease as the ridge-line and with an absolute minimum of PVA or glue-stick, fix it to the two triangle formers and to the two longer sides. Remember that this is only a dry run and, irrespective of its success or otherwise, it will have to be carefully removed.

You are now in a position to judge how accurate you have been in working out that all-important height and pitch of the roof. If it looks about right against your photographs, you can give yourself a pat on the back! If it looks too low and with too shallow a pitch, the solution is to re-cut the triangle formers to give a steeper pitch and higher ridge-line. Dismantle the piece and re-make it accordingly – it will only take a few minutes. Once you are satisfied that it is right, the next few steps are quite straightforward, although you do need to decide what form the roof slates will take. They will most likely be pre-prints or downloads in the most appropriate style and colour, but the most important the question concerns their thickness. If they are to be a pre-print, your roof will need to be extended to support the otherwise flimsy and vulnerable overhang. If, however, they are from a download and your printer will cope with thicker (100gsm) paper, then you can cut the roof right back to the eaves and allow just the slates to form the overhang.

If you settle on the former option, mark the mock-up accordingly with at least an extra 2mm extension beyond your ceiling. Having marked the front and rear (and remembering that the overhang extends beyond the corners), draw the diagonals that

The GWR made extensive use of blue brickwork as both a functional and decorative device. It is certainly an attractive feature but is tricky and somewhat tedious to capture in model form; this is one of the rare instances where extra magnification may be needed.

are the joins between the four segments of the roof; these are the lines from the corners to the ends of the ridge. These take care of the larger front and rear segments, but that still leaves the problem of the two shorter end segments.

THE FINAL STAGES

This next step is tricky rather than difficult. As it stands, there is a lot of surplus paper at each end and it all slopes the wrong way. It is time to carefully slit the paper along the two rear diagonals from the edge right up to the ends of the ridge. This has left the rear roof neatly intact and two large 'flaps' along the front. Very carefully score and bend these flaps along the other two diagonals, pushing them back until they rest against the ends of the rear roof. It is vital that these bends are 100 per cent accurate; they must appear to start at the ridge and maintain contact along the edges of the ceiling. Hold the flaps firmly in place, then draw what will be the cut lines where they rest against the rear roof.

If you are confident about your skill with the scalpel, make the cuts now, so that you can check that everything comes together correctly. Trim these two new templates to give the same 2mm overhang and then gently separate the whole piece from the

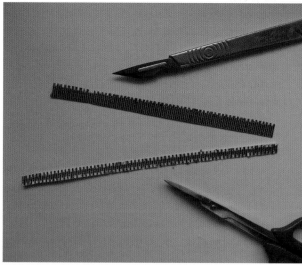

The original bricklayers simply incorporated the blue bricks as they went along, but the modeller has to produce them as overlays for gluing to the plinths, corners, doors and windows.

'ceiling'. Leave the completed template to one side for a moment as there is now one extra job that can be done on the 'ceiling' that will help the final assembly. The addition of ribs/formers to the two existing triangles will provide useful fixing points and make the detachable roof much stronger. One former sits along the centre-line between the triangles to support the ridge; the other four are identical 'right-angled triangles' running up from the corners to join at the ends of the ridge. These obviously secure the two bends at the front and the two joins at the rear. Make sure that all these items are securely fixed and properly upright.

The actual roof can now be cut from your chosen material using your proven template as a master. This can then be securely glued to the ceiling sub-assembly and set to one side to avoid damage. There is no need to slate it yet as you turn your attention back to the main structure.

WALLS AND WINDOWS

At this point you need to decide exactly which brick paper and glazing you are going to use. The style of brickwork used by the Great Western appears to be pretty consistent no matter where the box was located. It is described as 'Flemish Bond' and consists of alternate whole and half-bricks along each course; in bricklaying parlance, these are 'headers' and 'stretchers'. When you are trying to get the style right, and in the colour that is appropriate to your site, there are many alternative sources in either pre-print or download form. Research seems to indicate that the closest matches to Blue Anchor are BPB28 and BPB10 from Railway Scenics (although the latter is described as 'stretcher bond'); Howard Scenics also have an acceptable version. The readily available high-street offerings from Superquick and Metcalfe are the correct bond but may be a little too dark. However, everyone perceives colours differently, and this is further exacerbated by photographic reproductions, print quality and layout lighting. It is important always to make your own decision and select what looks best under your normal lighting conditions.

This project build used the Howard Scenics sheet and the B16 from True Texture for the decorative 'engineer's blue', together with whatever was available to match those very large slates. With respect to the glazing, one of the easiest options was to go for the sheet available from Prototype (46W7), currently marketed by Freestone Models. This contains several prints of the typical 'three-over-two' main windows, which are such a distinctive GWR trademark. It also includes a number of the smaller windows for the ground floor and doors. Its only disadvantage is that the glazing is relatively thin, and the bars and frames are just prints, lacking any relief.

It is worth doing as much basic painting and touching up as you can during the building process. The less you have to handle the completed model the better. It also helps you to get at areas that may prove inaccessible later.

Is it possible to find anything better and still remain within fairly simple construction methods? An extensive trawl through the web turned up nothing in either brass or wood frets, and only one possible in plastic as 'spares' from their signal box kit. So the Prototype glazing it is – particularly since this has stood the test of time in several boxes on my Wessex Lines for more than twenty years!

CREATING AND ASSEMBLING THE 'KIT'

The next decision is whether to opt for the score-and-bend assembly, keeping the artwork as one piece, or the butt-join method, with each elevation separated. The butt-join is easier to work with and, given the presence of the decorated corners, it will make it a simple task to disguise any imperfections. The first ask is to cut the artwork into the four individual walls. This requires some careful work with the scalpel, especially at what will be the two corners at the front of the box. The upper floor at these points is little more than an over-thick wooden window frames and the wooden eaves; at this stage they will need careful handling even if you intend to reinforce them later.

With the walls separated, you can now apply your paper of choice. The areas to cover are relatively small, so a glue-stick or glue-pen will be quite adequate. As always, do take special care to ensure that you avoid any wrinkles or bubbles and check that the paper is securely fixed to all the edges and apertures. Once you are satisfied that everything is ready, then each wall can be tidied up. Usually, the window and door apertures would be cut as diagonals, to enable the brick paper to be folded and fixed on the inside. However, since you will also have to accommodate the decorative blue brick, it is better to remove this first layer completely. The two shorter walls can retain a small strip at each end; this will be used to cover the join when the longer walls are glued in place.

DECORATIVE BRICKWORK

If there was ever any truth in the expression that 'the Devil is in the detail', for the modeller it must surely be in the GWR's use of 'engineer's blue'. Not content with just employing it to reinforce corners, doorways and windows, the company chose to make it into a trademark decorative style. Nor were they content just to feature half- and whole-brick steps

By this stage the model is really taking shape. The distinctive corbels have been fitted and the benefit of doing some basic interior detailing before final assembly is now very evident.

The false part-ceilings and the interior fittings, such as the lever frame, instrument shelf, cupboards and flower vases, ready for installing at the appropriate moment.

on alternate courses. Closer inspection reveals that even quarter-bricks were included! This poses two problems: first, how do you actually make such fiddly little details and, second, how do you disguise the fact that your overlays should really be an integral part of the main brickwork? One thing is certain, however: it cannot be ignored, as it is an essential element of the building's character.

There is no simple solution or easy procedure, but one way is to remove roughly 1mm squares from alternate courses while leaving the remaining 1mm squares undamaged. Exactly how you proceed will depend, to a large extent, on the keenness of your eye and the steadiness of your hand. In the latter case, you may well need an artificial aid to vision!

The procedure is as follows:

1) Keep the printed sheet intact for ease of handling and do ensure that the edge is cut absolutely straight, with the courses of whole bricks identified as remaining after cutting. You will be removing the alternate half-bricks.

2) Use very small, sharp scissors to 'nick' all the courses down the complete sheet.

3) Next, either bend up all the half-bricks into small 'tabs' and slice them off with the scalpel blade flat

to the surface. Alternatively, if you can, simply 'nick' them out on the cutting mat.

4) Lightly score the surface along the inner line of your whole bricks. The outer strip will become the visible decorative portion.

5) Finally, separate the strip a further two whole bricks in to give sufficient spare to fold through the apertures and secure to the back of the wall.

6) To disguise the obviousness of these overlays, at least partially, use a fine brush to touch in all the exposed edges; this is best done now before the items are stuck in position.

Use the photos as a guide and carefully cut the required number of courses to replicate the designs. There is no visible shading on the print so all the cuts can be done down the same side and the strip simply inverted to give the other side. Cut further individual bricks and fix them vertically to make the cornices above the apertures. This is a fairly lengthy (and tedious) task, but these decorative surrounds represent a vital aspect of the building's character.

While you are in the mood, this is a good time to continue the exercise and produce all the four strips destined for the corners: remember that these must be double-edged and the bricks must be removed

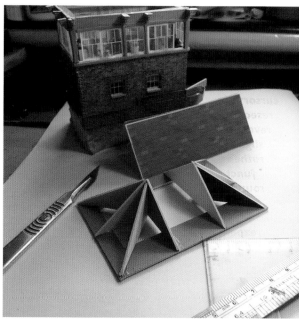

ALL IMAGES: *A hipped roof is one of the more difficult tasks facing the average modeller. It is essential to get the dimensions and angles correct, but there is no way of getting the real-life measurements. An easy and totally reliable method remains elusive and it invariably comes down to a mix of counting slates, using maths and geometry and trial-and-error paper mock-ups.*

The prominent ridge tiles at Blue Anchor are another example of the need for some ingenuity. Even the most cursory glance at the research photos will reveal that they are slightly decorative rather than purely functional. Their rounded top needs to be reproduced and some experiments with various thicknesses of paper are called for.

from the alternate courses on both sides. They are still only one whole brick wide on each side of the corner, so the eventual strips, either side of scored line, must have courses which run 'whole brick left, whole brick right, whole brick left', and so on. There are also blue-brick decorations to the large chimney breast at the rear of the box. Cut more than the measurements demand to make sure you have sufficient material to clad all the areas and with all the courses accurately aligned.

Keeping that last comment in mind, glue your blue-brick strips around the apertures, fixing to the outer wall sides first, then fold inwards, gluing as you go. Finally, glue any surplus to the inner wall. Where the windows are concerned, do make sure that everything is as taut and neat as possible before you fix the small glazings into place.

THE MAIN WINDOWS

The main windows are set into the wooden facia, so there is no brickwork to worry about, and they can be fixed to the inside of the mounting board. If it suits the season in which your layout is set, it would be a nice touch to have one or both of the sliding windows pulled open. Most of the pre-printed glazing sheets are quite thin and to get the relief effect it may

be worth experimenting with laminating an extra thickness of plastiglaze to the inside. However, there is a definite risk of creating unwelcome smears so do not attempt this unless you are confident and have done some test runs with scrap material. While the standard GWR 'three-over-two' windows may look the same, the dimensions of the actual panes will vary to fit different-sized apertures. Be prepared to do some careful surgery to achieve the optimum match.

WOODWORK AND FEATURES

Once the main windows are in place, you can turn your attention to the very distinctive woodwork and gutters. The area below the windows is relatively straightforward and is no more than a pronounced sill. Above the windows it is a different matter. The eaves take the form of a lip or shelf extending out from the top of the walls by about a foot (4mm). This is supported on an array of corbels, so you will need to invest in some suitable white-metal castings or attempt to carve them all from balsa wood. Fortunately, Dorset-based Scale Link Models, a manufacturer that produces signal-box interiors, also offers a wide range of detailing packs. These include other items that will be needed: the corbels, some square guttering and down-pipes and ventilators.

These white-metal packs have been around for some time and have been used to good effect on many layouts. Normally, it is necessary to prime the metal before applying its final finish. However, since these items do not need repeated handling, one under-coat of matt white enamel will stabilize the surface enough to take other enamels or even watercolours as a top coat.

The best method is to glue some decent-quality card of varying thicknesses to represent the plank-ing and window surrounds, then glue the corbels, ensuring their tops are flush with the top of the wall. Repeat these steps on the other three walls and put them aside to allow everything to dry nice and secure.

BRACING THE TOP OF THE BUILDING

Earlier, a base or semi-ceiling designed to fit the main structure exactly was incorporated into the roof assembly. It is now necessary to create something similar to help brace the top of the building, provide an optimum area on which to glue the roof (if it is not removable), and provide somewhere from which to hang the instrument shelf and diagram. As this has to go all around the box, it is a simple choice of cutting

it as another single 'hollow square'. This will sit tightly inside the tops of the walls, eliminating their inevi-table tendency to warp while also guaranteeing the 90-degree corners.

When drawing this out, the measurements need to be accurate. The sides of the rectangle should be at least 6mm wide taken from the inside of the walls. The instrument shelf and the signal-box diagram should be suspended from the ceiling but, with a detachable roof, this is simply not an option. You can provide fixing points for them by adding a small panel beneath the front-facing side. This will enable you to fix the shelf bracket without obscuring the detailing when the roof is removed; it is equally suitable for a fixed-roof option.

FINAL ASSEMBLY

Now all the key components are ready, you can assemble the front and side walls. A strong PVA would suffice but for jobs like this a clear glue such as UHU might be preferable, as it gives a little more time for adjustments. Always carry out this critical task on an absolutely flat surface – a glass-topped desk or table is ideal – and check repeatedly that the assembly is consistently square and vertical. Also ensure that the brick courses are accurately aligned:

The small entrance porch is a simple add-on, using the photos as a guide for its exact positioning.

The detailed interior can now be fitted and finalized, together with the part-ceiling on which the roof sub-assembly will be fixed.

the blue-brick decoration must be able to overlap the basic red, as if it were laid as a continuous exercise. Remember that the blue-brick plinth is slightly raised – use a strip of 0.75mm card from the back of a notepad.

When the glue is set, you take advantage of the absent rear wall to measure, cut and fit the floor. You might want to fit two floors, with the second hidden towards the bottom of the walls and fitted first. At this point, you can either glue the top floor in place and complete the detailing with it in situ, or you can make up the floor as a fully detailed sub-assembly prior to inserting it. The latter is probably preferable. The detailing kits are full of tiny components and these are much easier to paint when fixed in position on an easily accessible false floor. This is certainly better than trying to do them held in tweezers and juggled into their correct positions. Remember that it will only be the backs of the instruments that can be glimpsed through the windows.

DETAILING THE INTERIOR

This project demonstrates that it is perfectly possible to create a 'cheap-n-cheerful' interior in just a couple of hours, using scrap card, micro-rod and bits

The steps are now fitted and the gutters, down-pipes and roof can be glued in place.

of plastic – the only concession is a ModelU 'bobby'. The end result would be more than adequate for any fixed-roof signal box.

The interior kits from Springside (white-metal) and Ratio (plastic) both contain a sufficient number of parts to enable the modeller to detail even a comparatively large and busy box. It goes without saying that not all of them will be needed for the Blue Anchor box; equally, some other items will need to be scratch-built. Some features are obviously more recent additions, reflecting the needs of a volunteer-run tourist railway that is obliged to follow the stringent safety regimes of the early twenty-first century. For the project, the aim was to strike a balance and create an interior that would not look out of place either in the present day or in the steam era proper.

It is best, but not essential, to use the card for the floor dark side uppermost, since the first task is to paint it to represent brown linoleum. A satin brown enamel would be ideal; otherwise, use a matt dark brown and give it a thin coat of gloss varnish.

- **Lever frame:** once it is dry, cut the frames to seventeen slots, to give enough for the fourteen levers and some spare, and glue them centrally across the box about 10mm in from the front wall. Give the frames a thin coat of metallic black or 'gunmetal' – either will do. Not all the levers require the wire tensioners (these are usually only necessary for the outermost signals), but they are evident behind the furthest ones at the 'up' end of the frame. Glue them into place and paint them with satin black. Make the capstan-wheel assembly and glue it in place at the right of the frame. This should also be painted in satin black, with the handles left as bare metal.

- **Levers:** the levers should be painted as follows: red (home or stop signals), yellow (distant signals), black (points), blue (facing-point locks), brown (gates/lever frame release) and white (spare levers). The levers are always arranged to mirror the respective positions of their signals when viewed from the box. In the case of Blue Anchor, reading from the left or 'up' side, the sequence is white, red, red, white, white, blue/white, blue/black, white, white, white, black, red, red, red, white, brown, brown and with two further blue levers in the far right-hand corner. These very small items are best painted before being inserted in the frame. They will take enamels but, if you do not have those colours to hand, they can be painted in matt white and

The box is now ready for siting at the platform end of the GWR station. Note that it still sits on its extra depth foundations for an open-top baseboard, this can be carved off if not required.

The completed project poses at Knighton Yard on 'Wessex Lines', with a kit-built BR 3MT tank and goods train disguising those extra foundations.

then the individual levers can be picked out with dense watercolours. The levers can then be set in the frame and fixed with superglue. Do not rush this and make sure all the 'on' levers are correctly aligned. Refer to the photos and have some in the 'off' position to reinforce the impression of activity. As a final touch, a quick coat of chrome enamel to their handles may help them appear more visible through the windows.

- **Furniture:** using the photographs as a guide, you can now start placing the various cupboards, chair, stool, desks, stove and token instruments. These are probably large enough to paint in situ, but doing them first may give a better result. There are quite a few other items which are not covered by the kit, but would add to the homely character of the box. It is up to you how far you go in pursuit of accuracy. Thin card or paper will be the best medium unless you are a dab hand with plastic scraps.

- **Instruments:** finally, you can assemble the instrument shelf and paint as much of the detail as your eyesight and steady hand will permit. Use superglue to attach it to the supports, pre-painted with matt black and trimmed to give the correct height, and then fix the supports to your portion of false ceiling.

If you have got that last bit right, you can push the completed floor assembly into place and clear-glue it to the three walls. It should be roughly 30in below the window sills and with the levers clear of the shelf. The final touch is to add the vital signal-box diagram beneath the ceiling – this need be no more than a finely drawn outline on a piece of thin card. If the back can be glimpsed from outside, pre-paint it matt black.

The interior is now complete and the back wall can be glued in place ready for you to finish off the exterior details.

COMPLETING AND PAINTING THE EXTERIOR

Like many signal boxes, Blue Anchor has undergone a few changes in its lifetime. One of the most obvious is the porch which protects the small veranda. Anyone who has visited the area when the rain is coming in on a stiff 'Nor-Easter' off the Bristol Channel will be in little doubt as to the reason behind this addition! It can be quickly constructed from thin card, using the photographs as a guide and to calculate the dimensions. If you are re-siting the box somewhere less exposed, you could dispense with this and use the images of Crowcombe as your reference.

The access steps are equally simple to fabricate or you may wish to explore the kit websites to see if they are offered anywhere as a spare.

The final tasks before reaching for the paint pots are adding and fixing the remainder of the blue-brick, finishing the chimney stack, and positioning the ventilator. All of this is quite straightforward, as long as you continue to refer to the illustrations of the model and the photographs of the real thing.

Painting should also be straightforward. The photos show the paint scheme that is correct for the preservation period and for its GWR origins. For its post-1948 time under BR(W), cream and brown should be substituted for the current 'light and dark stone'.

ABOVE, RIGHT AND OPPOSITE: A series of general and detail images for modellers who would like to make their own version but may not be able to visit this corner of Somerset.

THE WILLITON SIGNAL BOX

The choice of Williton for a project build was based on the same evaluation as that undertaken for the Blue Anchor exercise. However, there were some additional factors that contributed to the decision. The box is certainly 'small and compact'; it is an example of a contractor's work for a pre-grouping company and is acknowledged to be the last working survivor from the Bristol and Exeter Railway. It is also interesting in its use of more local materials in its construction. One final point in its favour is the fact that, while it too controls a level-crossing, this is a much more minor installation, with gates that are manually opened by the duty signalman. All these things added together make it a perfect project for the branch-line modeller.

FIELD RESEARCH AND DIMENSIONS

Research was relatively easy, with good access from all the necessary angles; it is even possible to photograph the roof, thanks to the fairly recently installed footbridge! The entire survey took less than a couple of hours and that included a generous invitation to view and record the interior. While you are on site, it makes sense to photograph all the other items that you may decide to include in the day. Possible subjects might be point-rodding and signal wires, signals, the level-crossing, adjacent buildings/structures and telephone connections. Since digital photography is so simple and carries little by way of extra costs, it is no hardship to snap everything in sight.

Once you are back at your desk or work-bench, you can start to develop the results of your trip into the finished artwork. Load all the images on to the laptop and select those that will be the most useful in the design of the kit. These will obviously include all those that show the very basic measuring-stick. Print them off as A4 sheets and then prepare a sketch, together with the key information and dimensions, from which the final artwork can be drawn on to the thin card and foamboard carcass.

Following the methods described earlier should result in a 'kit' that measures 56mm by 70mm, with

The second project is historically significant as it the last Bristol & Exeter Railway signal box that is still fully operational. A field visit yielded the necessary clutch of images, many of which included the 4-ft measuring-stick to calculate the dimensions.

As always, the creation of sketches and working drawings is essential if the final build is to proceed satisfactorily.

The basic medium this time is normal foamboard, obtainable from most dealers and hobby shops. It is easy to work but does demand a sharp scalpel and vertical cuts through its 5mm (actually nearer 7mm!) thickness. You can still scribble on it, albeit only with a ballpoint or felt-tip pen.

Construction principles are virtually the same as they are with card. In this case it is the gable ends that are cut to the full dimensions, with the front and back walls reduced to fit.

The brickwork, dating from the mid-1800s, is not easy to reproduce but some off-cuts from the bits box appear near enough for the project. The lower floor is mounting board, which gave the required element of relief.

Glazing came from a pre-printed sheet and was not 100 per cent correct. Some tweaking was required to make it fit into the dimensionally accurate apertures.

A box of watercolours is ideal for making subtle changes to brick or tiles as well as for touching in exposed edges. The back wall is still separate at this stage in order to get at the glazing, which is push-fit and must be fixed at the front of the aperture almost flush with the outside of the walls.

a maximum height of 80mm to the top of the gable ends. One thing to be aware of from the outset is the need to plot ground level as a horizontal from the lowest visible point. This will enable you to build the model as free-standing on an open site, or to continue with the prototype, which is part-concealed by the platform. You may also wish to extend your artwork to a given depth below ground level for a hidden foundation within the baseboard.

As always, there is the inevitable question of interior detail. On the positive side the operating floor is small and boasts a lot of original nineteenth-century fixtures and fittings, notably the neat little kitchen range in the corner, which makes a welcome change from the more usual free-standing stoves. There is, however, an unavoidable negative in that the interior is quite gloomy, due to the relatively limited window area. One option would be to make it viewable, with either a detachable roof or fully removable rear wall and floor. It is probably best to proceed with the main structure and re-examine the options when the box is closer to final assembly.

This structure has some quite unusual brickwork. The decorative quoins and other features, which you would normally expect to encounter as 'engineer's blue', are in fact a very pale almost grey brick. Indeed, it could easily be mistaken for dressed stonework. If that were not enough of a challenge, there is also very pronounced staining or weathering of the main brickwork. There are also two 'plinths' – the rear of the box stands on a stone-built extension of the platform – as well as a further plinth that carries the operating floor. These aspects will demand no little ingenuity when it comes to the exterior finish, including a subtle combination of brick paper and watercolour paints.

There is one very prominent item that you might think you could ignore unless you were modelling the preservation era. This is the large 'running-in board' mounted on the back wall. After all, this would surely have been most unlikely to have existed anywhere during the days of the former companies or the nationalized railways? Wrong! In fact, it shows up very clearly in photographs of some evacuees arriving at the station early in the war.

THIS PAGE AND OVERLEAF: *The building sits in a rather complex series of levels – the actual setting can prove to be as important as the building itself, especially if you compound the problem by adding a foundation.*

DRAWING AND ASSEMBLING

The first step is to translate your sketch plan and scribbled notes into usable artwork. The procedure is exactly the same as for the Blue Anchor box and resulting drawings only differ in respect of the gable ends. At Williton, you will need to take account of the ridge-style roof and that does demand particular care in getting the two gable ends not only accurate but also absolutely identical. If those walls are wrong, then the roof will not fit – and you do not want to discover such an error when it is too late!

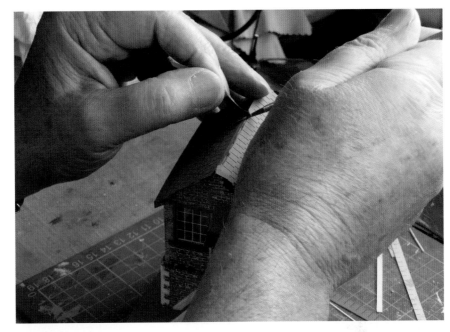

TOP AND BOTTOM:
The ridge tiles at Williton are also slightly out of the ordinary, as they have a small spine running along the top. This is fairly easy to replicate by folding a length of pre-print strip along its centre line, re-opening it, then gluing one half slightly higher up the roof than usual. Using tweezers on both sides of the strip, pinch a small spine, then glue the strip in a similar position. Continue to pinch along the ridge until it resembles the subject.

The model of Williton occupying the site at Knighton Yard, with a tank wagon hiding the extra depth of the foundations and platform. It is a neat little building and could easily be put to use anywhere in the West Country.

The big difference is that ridge-style roofs need to be considered as 'integral' components with the walls. Hipped roofs can be designed and built quite separately from the basic structure, as they sit on the base of the false ceiling, and you need do no more than ensure that your supporting walls are square and level. Do not be intimidated by the care and accuracy that are required; as long as you apply all the necessary details and dimensions correctly, the job will be right first time. There is one tip that is worth following: as well as double-checking your artwork before you wield your scalpel, take a few minutes with some card off-cuts to test your plan.

This does not involve much effort. All that will be needed is a corner section of the front wall and the gable end up to the ridge-line and a further piece of card to represent the eventual roof template. Offer them up in the way you intend for the final assembly – if it all fits neatly together, you will know that it is safe to proceed. If it does not, then you will be able to identify and correct the problem.

The key point to remember is that the decision in respect of the corners is critical. Both the score-and-bend and the butt-joint methods work equally well, but they demand different measurements and different fixings for the roof template. (See the drawings in Appendix I.)

THIS AND PAGES 170–71: *A selection of images to help the modeller who wants to try Williton as a project. The two roof shots will hopefully endorse the argument over zero-thickness tiles when viewed from any distance.*

CORFE CASTLE SIGNAL BOX

This is another example of a box that is well suited to scratch-building and is of particular appeal to those modellers intending to site it towards the back of a layout. This is because the rear is difficult to access for photographs and is, in any case, fairly uninteresting. Historically, the box is not quite what it seems. Although it appears to feature in the many period images of Corfe Castle station, it is in fact a twenty-first-century reconstruction and the result of many years of dedicated effort by the volunteers on the Swanage Railway.

The structure is readily accessible for research and measurement, and is a good example of a box built on a public platform. Another 'plus' is the fact that it is largely of timber construction; because of this, it can justifiably (and very conspicuously) carry the house styles of the LSWR, SR and BR(S) from the 1920s to the present day.

The drawing and assembly processes are exactly the same as for the two previous examples. The main difference will be in the final stages of the finish, when

Some of the results from the initial field-research visit to Corfe Castle on the Swanage Railway. The eventual model will be a companion piece to a scratch-built goods shed and engine shed.

The third project uses a new basic material: balsa wood. This was relatively well known to modellers in the 1950s and early 60s, but the growth of plastics in sheet and strip form, together with the increased availability of good-quality card, soon pushed it aside.

you will have to decide exactly how to reproduce those quite substantial wooden planks. You could of course search out a suitable builder's aid, in pre-print, download, plastic sheet or even laser-cut, but you might like to see what you can do on your own work-bench using the traditional balsa wood in its many forms. The exercise may tax both your skill and your ingenuity, but it should help you to experience the great satisfaction that can be had from scratch-building.

You may also need to purchase, paint or fabricate those very distinctive 'trademark' windows, as well as card for those several hundred clay tiles.

The attractive operating floor just begs to be modelled, so the removable-back version with the

Balsa is very easy to cut – indeed it is almost too easy when working with the grain. Score-and-bend corners are not an option, so these are the four walls suitably trimmed to give nice clean corners while still maintaining the correct external dimensions.

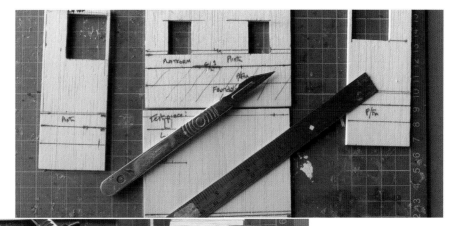

Corfe box is wood-planked on a brick plinth, in a very traditional form of construction that can be seen on the most ancient of wooden barns. If machine-cut hardwood strips for the planks are not available, they may be scalpel-cut from the 1/16th sheet of balsa wood. it's worth using your setsquare to rule some guidelines to help you keep the planks horizontal.

The planking is done and has been trimmed (maintaining the snug fit on the corners) and the initial coat of paint applied.

floor attached is a good option. A word of warning: the box is built on a small embankment and access to the locking room is at this lower level. To simplify things and to make the project more suitable for general use, this normally unseen area has not been modelled. Those who are building the box in its proper location will need to undertake some extra independent research. Those distinctive bonnet tiles will also present quite a challenge.

Another instance of the glazing needing to be a push-fit into the apertures. This will make painting difficult, so do it now prior to the glazing exercise.

STARTING POINT

Once again, start with a few A4 prints and sketch out the general appearance and key dimensions. Basing your calculations on the mix of data from the measuring-stick and the brick count will yield an approximate length of 25ft (100mm) and an apparent width of 12ft 6in (50mm), without too much compromise. Working to 13ft 6in (54mm) would probably produce a better result, but this will have some implications in respect of the width of the proposed platform. There must be an absolute minimum of 6ft (24mm) between the front of the signal box and the platform edge. There is however some flexibility over where the boundary fence should fall, and to what extent, if any, the box might project beyond it. This need not concern you on this actual exercise, but it is something to be considered by modellers who intend to install the box on their layout.

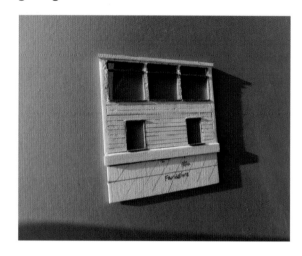

Another benefit from doing one wall at a time – any attempt to deal with the frames later will be much more difficult.

DRAWING AND ASSEMBLING

Take a section of balsa large enough to contain all the artwork, but still small enough to be easily manageable on your desk. Sheet balsa is usually available in 36 x 4in pieces and you will need two thicknesses – 1/16th and 1/32nd – plus some lengths of 1/16th strip. The material is very easy to work and requires less effort than card, as a sharp scalpel will simply slide through even the thicker sheets. As before, you will need an HB pencil, a ballpoint pen, a ruler and a set-square and either a pair of dividers or a digital Vernier scale. The process is no more complicated than making an accurate transcription of your rough design as a piece of proper artwork ready to be cut out. Keep your original photo prints close at hand to check any details and resolve any issues.

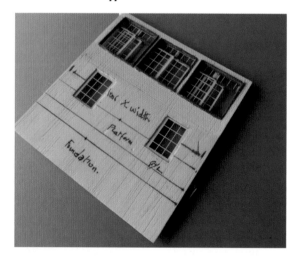

The finished model will include a detailed interior so you will also need to reproduce the paintwork on the inner walls and frames.

Another troublesome hipped roof demands some more maths and trial and error. The covering this time is clay tiles so you will need cut your own strips or locate something suitable from one of the suppliers of builder's aids.

Roof assembly and tiling can be done in several ways. The key thing is to make a base that will give exactly the right dimensions, including that pronounced overhang. The tile strips can be fixed to each portion of the roof before assembly; they can be applied to the assembled roof; or they can be glued to 80gsm copier paper and treated like a sheet of pre-print.

LEFT, BELOW AND OPPOSITE: *The distinctive bonnet tiles are an essential feature on Corfe's roof, as on many other red-roofed buildings. They are notoriously difficult to capture in miniature. They must be laid individually at the joins of each course, they must overlap equally from bottom to top – and in this scale, they measure barely 4mm across and 5mm deep – and they are slightly curved. And the modeller does not have the option of holding them in place with cement! Experiments with various weights of card and paper, secured with different adhesives, failed to achieve an acceptable result. The last resort was to cut a child's drinking straw in half vertically, chop it into the required 5mm lengths and shape one end into a rough triangle, and secure the pieces with Deluxe Glue 'n' Glaze. It will be frustrating and time-consuming and you may prefer to abandon the idea and stick to simple ridge tiles.*

The entrance porch and stairs are the usual basically simple but time-consuming task; you need do little more than follow your photographs and offer up the work to make sure of it.

Score-and-bend is no longer an option, so it will be butt-joint corners and the possible introduction of wood-strip or even plastic for those conspicuous corner posts. This is real-world kit design and the only rules will be those that you choose to follow for your own ends. Over time, you will develop your own almost instinctive methods and short-cuts, mostly through good old-fashioned trial and error. The materials are cheap and your modelling time is not costed, so do not be too concerned if you make mistakes. All you will have at the beginning is a knowl-

edge of your intended destination, so think of it as an voyage of discovery, and just press on until you get something satisfactory.

The Corfe Castle box is another example of the hipped-roof style and the false-ceiling or roof-base approach described for the Blue Anchor box should apply equally to this design. The only difference is in the finish; unusually, it has clay tiles, with bonnet tiles covering the four hips. This is another sound reason for including this example here, as it will introduce new problems and their possible solutions.

Corfe's detailed interior is permanently attached to the removable back wall. The figures are the more recently introduced range from ModelU.

Finished at last, with its name-board cut from one of the photos, the box is re-sited at ground level, substituting for Sherborne 'A' signal box on 'Wessex Lines'.

The construction is not very different from the previous card exercises. Always keep your main printed references close to hand, together with quick access to your laptop for any detail shots you have taken for back-up. Make constant use of offering up and do not be afraid to experiment, especially if this is your first time with balsa wood.

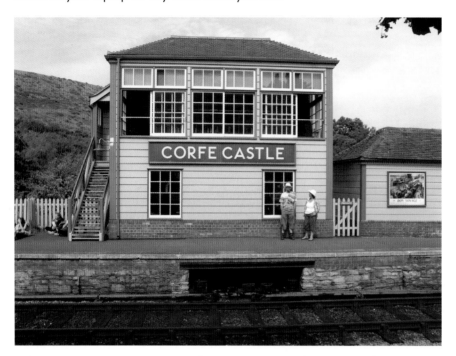

PAGES 181–183: *General and detail shots for modellers who want a typical LSWR box for their layout. For those with a site like the real Corfe, there are a couple of images that hint at the rear of the box. For good measure, the section closes, with roof-top views and a final shot of the dreaded bonnet tiles.*

CONCLUSIONS

Despite the plethora of kits in the various mediums, and the many subtle ways in which they may be improved or customized, please do consider taking up the challenge and having a go at scratch-building. It is a much lengthier process than assembling an off-the-shelf kit, but for sheer job-satisfaction it is without equal; the sense of achievement you get when seeing your own finished work on your layout is surely what modelling is all about.

My very first attempt at scratch-building dates from 1972 and is a model of the cottage that was our former home in Shap village. It still graces my 'Wessex Lines' layout and continues to give me a 'buzz', especially knowing that it was the model that

began everything that I went on to achieve in the ensuing decades. You will inevitably make mistakes but these are all part of the learning process; they are more than counterbalanced by the opportunity to discover a technique or material that will makes life better or easier.

Prepare as thoroughly as you can, but never be afraid to depart from your original ideas; as Winston Churchill declared, 'Flexibility is the fourth dimension of planning!' If something really is not working, find an alternative approach. If something new suggests itself, then capitalize on it. Above all, enjoy the work for its own sake and, if it becomes too stressful or a chore, then go on your layout and watch the trains go round, or nip into your model shop and spend a few bob on that resin ready-to-site alternative.

CHAPTER EIGHT

AN OVERVIEW OF SIGNALS AND SIGNALLING

THE ORIGINS OF SEMAPHORE SIGNALS

The earliest railways were controlled, if that is the word, not by signals but by top-hatted railway policemen. Their equipment was no more elaborate than a reliable timepiece, a copy of the timetable and some flags or a whistle to convey their instructions to the approaching trains. The basic concept of 'green for go', 'yellow for caution' and 'red for danger' was about as sophisticated as things could get. The hazards associated with this system are certainly obvious to our contemporary eyes and must have soon become apparent to our Victorian forebears. Given the inevitable unreliability of the early locomotives and their consequent inability to maintain any sort of strict timetable (or, indeed, even to complete their journey at all), the policeman's reliance on a given time interval before displaying his green flag to a following train was at best optimistic.

It is a miracle that there were not a lot more accidents and that the railways flourished and developed in the way that they did. Something clearly had to be done as trains were growing ever more numerous, more frequent and heavier and faster. Someone would have to come up with a workable idea and a wholly practical solution to a problem that had never previously been encountered. It needed a genius – an inventor with vision as well as a solid grasp of current technology. Step forward, Isambard Kingdom Brunel.

Synonymous with the Great Western Railway, Brunel not only dreamed of steam travel from London to New York and trains capable of eighty miles an hour, he would also become one of the fathers of mechanical signalling. His idea, albeit much enhanced by later engineers, would be employed world-wide and continue in use to the present day. The system has come a long way from his original disc and bar signals, but, whatever railway or region you choose to model, when you place your signals on the layout it is right to pay silent tribute to the brilliant man and his fellows. All that went before became obsolete, apart from the nickname of the generations of signalmen who followed the railway policemen – they were and still are known as 'bobbies'!

THE BASICS OF MECHANICAL SIGNALLING

This vast and complex subject cannot be covered here in any great detail, but there are a few key areas that are relevant to modellers when planning, building and installing our signals. There are a host of books and articles that can guide those in search of more information on this fascinating topic, but a grasp of some basic principles will help you to avoid some of the more common errors.

Perhaps the most obvious point is that signals are there to protect the train in front rather than ease the passage of a following service. Even where signals are sited before a junction, level-crossing, point-work or station, their function is still the same: to protect that particular installation. Any engineman whose Bank Holiday express to the West Country is already an hour down at Exeter, due to late-running services in front, will soon tell you about this protection business.

(See the illustrations and diagrams in Appendix II.)

DESCRIPTIONS AND FUNCTIONS

Looking first at the simple mechanical type of signals, they must clearly show the three simple instructions, 'stop', 'caution' and 'go'. They must be unambiguous

and visible from some distance, both by day and at night. It may be a legacy from the original policemen, but some form of 'arm' is the obvious solution with the inclusion of a lamp at night. If the arm is extended horizontally, it clearly represents a barrier to further progress, and means 'stop'. Add a red light in some way and that conveys the same instruction in the dark or in poor light. If the arm is then raised or lowered, that is an indication that the barrier has gone and it is safe to proceed; a green light is the solution when it is dark.

The question of proceeding with caution and being prepared to stop is more difficult to convey. If anything, it is actually easier by night when an amber or yellow warning light can be used. By day, an intermediate position for the arm does not work as well. It is simply not sufficiently unambiguous and is too easy to be misread as 'go'. The answer was to colour the arms but to use a different colour and introduce a different shape to show 'caution'.

The arms were placed on top of a tall post and operated by wires running from a central building or 'box'. All the basic elements were now in place. Since these moving arms were similar in concept to the principles of the military flags used in semaphore-signalling, and since most of the inspecting officers on the railways were ex-military men, this system was naturally given that same name. The 'stop' signals were made with square ends and painted red, while 'caution' signals were made with vee-shaped (or fish-tail) ends and painted yellow. The solution to the lighting problem owed something to the theatrical profession, where coloured shades were placed over ordinary white lights to change their aspect. On the railway signals, the lamps were attached to the post immediately behind the arm, which now included red (or orange) and turquoise glass shades. The final, and perhaps the most significant feature, was that all signals were designed to return to the horizontal 'stop' position at all times, even in the event of breakages or failures.

Although these basic principles were taken up by all the companies, and indeed by all other countries, there were several different interpretations. The most obvious and longest-lasting would be the position of the arm when showing 'off' or 'proceed'. Some railways chose to allow the signal to drop down to an angle of around 45 degrees using balance

Another example from the Swanage Railway, the up 'splitting home' signal at Harmans Cross. Like most intermediate stations on single-track branch lines, it is bi-directional and either platform can be used for up or down workings.

weights to return it back to the 'on/stop' position. This is known as 'lower-quadrant' signalling and was favoured by the LNWR, LSWR and GWR, among others. The alternative, which was chosen by the LNER, SR and their constituent companies, had the arms raised at a similar angle in the 'off' position; this is known as the 'upper-quadrant' type.

BLOCK SIGNALLING

How was mechanical semaphore-signalling used in the steam era, and beyond? The concept is quite simple, even if the eventual development of the railways did lead to quite complex interpretations. It all stems from that first principle of protecting the train or installation ahead. The track, be it a single-line branch or a particular running-line on a major trunk route, is divided into sections or 'blocks'. If a block is clear of any traffic, then the signal protecting it is pulled 'off' and a train is allowed into it. The signal is then returned to the 'on' or 'stop' position, to prevent the next working from entering and possibly hitting the rear of the first. There is no set rule for the length of a block but it must be capable of holding one complete train, at least. When there is a succession of blocks, each protected by its own 'stop' or 'home' signal, those same signals can also serve the same purpose as those found at the departure end of a platform – except that they would not be called 'starters', as in station terminology.

If this is getting a bit confusing, the diagrams in Appendix II should help to clarify things.

The second type of arm, the 'caution' or 'distant' yellow version, is there to warn the enginemen that, while they are clear to pass it even though it is in the 'on' or 'stop' position and enter the block, they must be aware that the one beyond may still be obstructed and that its protecting 'home' signal may be set at 'stop'. Should the distant arm be 'off', this indicates that both this block and the one beyond are clear.

It is very rare to find both 'home' and 'distant' arms on the post on a single-track branch line. This is, however, a very commonplace occurrence on multi-track mainlines. In all such cases, the 'distant' is always placed below the 'home'. The situation can arise where the block controlled by the 'advanced starter' for box A is also under the control of the 'distant' for box B. It is easy to see how 'A' is happy to allow a train to leave his section and pulls his signal 'off', while 'B' is happy to accept it but only under caution and therefore leaves his distant signal 'on'. The implication is that he still has a previous working in his section and may wish to protect it with his 'outer-home'.

There are a couple of other quite common applications that can be used to good effect by the modeller. The first is found on busier branch lines, where the blocks actually relate to the junction, the intermediate stations and the eventual terminus. Most services will be required to stop at all of the

A typical starting signal with a short post located at the end of the platform for ease of sighting by the footplate crew.

stations so the advance warning, in the familiar form of a 'distant' signal, is provided. However, since the need to prepare to stop is virtually a constant, this signal can be kept as non-working and permanently 'on'. These are known as 'fixed-distants'.

SUBSIDIARY SIGNALS

Another type of signal with a very specific function, and therefore restricted to a limited type of location, is the 'shunt signal'. The design may vary from region to region but they will all be based on the standard 'home' or 'starter' arm. Among the easiest to spot is the GWR version, which consists of a short (four-foot) arm carrying a round white hoop. The purpose of the shunt signal was to allow limited access to a block as part of further movement. In other words,

it would enable an engine to draw forward in order to then set back into a siding, loop or bay to deposit or retrieve additional vehicles. Such signals could occasionally be found in quite large numbers where groups of sidings could not be properly shunted without frequent forays on to a running-line.

The final signals to mention are the 'calling-on' arm and the 'backing-signal', both of which are self-explanatory. At busy mainline stations, a single signal might well give approval to several different movements, which would be shown on an integrated 'route indicator'. This was generally known to footplate men as the 'cash register', due to its similarity in operation and appearance to those contraptions found on the counters of the traditional shops.

Last but certainly not least in terms of numbers are the 'ground' or 'shunting-disc' signals. These are

Knighton Yard on 'Wessex Lines' provides two examples of subsidiary signals: the 42xx waits at the backing signal with its cash-register indicator; further over, the four-arm shunting signal controls access from the sidings.

Two examples of standard ground signals, with the Southern version carrying the pale grey paintwork and ex-GWR in black. Note that both have balance weights. Such signals have the same authority as a post-mounted 'stop' arm.

simply a cheap and effective method of controlling relatively short movements within the environs of a station or yard. They serve exactly the same purpose as the post-mounted shunt or calling-on arm and are usually found in the six-foot on the driver's side. Because they are unobtrusive and virtually impossible to mistake or misread, they are a far more practical answer than the whole forest of signal posts that they replace. However, at busy stations and where the normally sited disc would be on a platform, they are often combined with the other arms on a bracket signal and sometimes even on a simple single arm starter. There is a prototype for everything if you look hard enough!

REFERENCES

Having looked at signalling on the real railway, it is time to consider how it might be reproduced on a layout. There are a number of ways in which signals can be correctly sited to 'perform' their allotted functions and yet still fulfil an additional role as attractive and realistic scenic accessories.

Photographic albums will always be a source of inspiration and prototype information. In addition to that, you can use your own camera on the tourist lines and preserved railways. This of course has the additional advantage of enabling you to record all the details, from several angles, which will be of great assistance when you get back to the modelling bench. There are also numerous online sites, including geograph.org.uk and signalbox.org, which will provide you with hundreds of images from all over the country; just search on 'railway semaphore signals'. Many of the photos also include good views of the signal boxes, which is an added bonus.

For other useful references, see Appendix III.

IMPROVING YOUR SIGNALLING

USING SIGNALLING CORRECTLY

Most modellers' layouts feature far too many signals – they are a bit addictive and you can blame those manufacturers whose kits are too attractive and too hard to resist. Even if you are only modelling a humble

branch-line terminus, and could therefore make do with just a couple of 'home' (stop) signals and a fixed-distant, the kit will probably include all sorts of other lovely bits, which it would be a shame to discard. As a result, many modellers end up with an array of signals that would be better suited to a busy mainline junction!

There is another, perhaps more reasonable, explanation for over-signalling, and that is their undoubted role as scenic accessories. They make an invaluable contribution to any layout, echoing their presence in the thousands of photographs from the prototype albums. Modeller's licence and the art of compromise allow you to include signals, albeit the correct type, for their scenic effect, irrespective of the fact that they are much too close together.

This may seem to be the antithesis of using signals correctly, but the trick, if there is one, is to make certain that each signal and every post is accurately modelled and is properly placed for its precise purpose against your track plan. If you study some of the images of 'Wessex Lines', you will immediately judge that the stations, junctions and signal boxes are actually only a few feet apart rather than the several

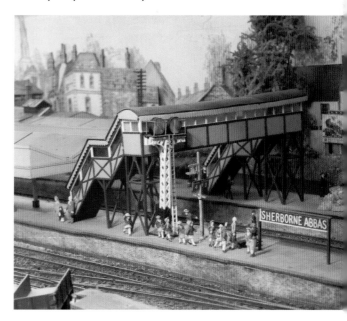

Something different: this Sykes banner repeater not only adds interest but is also correctly sited to 'repeat' the positions of the up starters obscured by Sherborne's extensive canopies.

yards that would have been demanded on a true-to-scale version of the real world. In the same vein, signals that should have had many hundreds of yards between them are often less a train's length away. However, their purpose is still clearly defined and their scenic contribution for the viewer or through the viewfinder is undeniable.

Having run out of excuses for malpractice, you need to revisit some of the basics for correct signalling; see Appendix II for diagrams that illustrate some of the fundamentals. Use the references to prepare plans for your existing or envisaged layouts. This is best done early on, but the cost of signal kits, and indeed of signal boxes, is relatively low, so even a complete replacement programme should not break the bank. There is no attempt at scale – the diagrams show simple track plans with the appropriate signals described – but they should provide enough information to enable the layout planner to decide which signals are needed. Those whose systems are already up and running will be able to revisit their scheme to make sure it is suitably 'prototypical'.

LEFT OR RIGHT?

The final point is invariably somewhat contentious: which side of the running-lines should you place your signal posts? Unfortunately, there is no simple and universal answer to the question. The most common siting seems to be to the left of the track with the doll or arm facing outwards. On most regions this could be described as the 'driver's side'; however, that will not fit the Great Western, with its right-hand-drive locomotives. This time it is the fireman who must help his mate and, when he can, watch for the road. There will also be instances where signal posts have to swap sides, in order to maintain the proper sight-lines on curves. Also, again in GWR territory, there will be instances where the original broad-gauge track-bed has left adequate room for signals to be sited between the running-lines.

The best advice is to study the appropriate steam albums for your chosen area and see how the real Signal & Telegraph engineers went about their business. See also 'Recommended Reading'.

Torpoint's up advanced starter and distant are on the wrong side to ease the view around the curves of the South Devon coast. The back-boards are there to block out the distracting background – in this case the young ladies from the nearby St Trinians Academy!

APPEARANCE

Most experienced modellers have their own pet hates when it comes to studying other people's layouts. When it comes to signals, ready-made or kit-built, it seems to me that there is an all too frequent lack of any form of safety protection. This is particularly conspicuous on gantries but even single-arm posts often omit the mandatory 'hoops'. The sad thing is that so many modellers have worked hard, and not without cost, to make their signals operate and yet leave them utterly devoid of this vital feature. The task is rather fiddly and the resultant end product can be somewhat fragile, but if you want a railway that looks right this particular nettle must be firmly grasped. Follow the step-by-step approach, which is hopefully well within the scope of even a newcomer to the hobby, and requires no more technology than a simple pin vice, scalpel and solvent, together with a supply of 0.50mm/0.020in plastic rod.

INSPIRATION FROM THE PROTOTYPE

As with all customizing (kit-bashing) or scratch-building, this task starts with research. Once again it requires very little effort. Go through your albums

The up splitting home for Crowcombe's platforms shows the quite complex steelwork typical of this later-style GWR installation.

Knighton's down starter is inspired by a similar and much-photographed example at Llanvihangel on the borders line from Hereford to Shrewsbury.

The 28xx is held at Knighton's distinctive shunt signal; the real version used to grace the yard at Abergavenny.

and magazines and seek out examples of signals fulfilling the same roles as those you want to model. Make some quick sketches or mark the pages, but make sure those you prefer are actually suitable and appropriate to your chosen site.

It is good practice to keep a permanent scrap-pad or notebook constantly close at hand whenever you enjoy the luxury of a good browse or devour the latest magazine. Whenever you spot something that you like, just jot it down, even if it is only an ultra-simple matchstick drawing. Almost every signal on 'Wessex Lines' and 'East Ilsley' came from sketches of things that 'might come in handy one day'.

OPTIONS

SINGLE-ARM 'HOME' OR 'STOP' SIGNALS

Single-arm 'home' or 'stop' signals are available from most high-street model shops in a choice of at least three formats: a ready-to-site version from Hornby

(rather loosely LMS/BR in design and currently priced at £10); several designs in familiar Ratio kits (available in accurately modelled types for all the major companies/BR regions); and lastly 'quick-assembly' working models, also from Ratio. There may be others but these are the most common and the most likely to be seen on other people's layouts. A newer entry from Dapol is available but this is electrically operated and, with a price tag of just under £30, is not really suitable for customizing.

THE HORNBY SIGNAL

This really is old-fashioned Hornby (or Triang) and is nearer to the toy market than it is to modelling. However, it is out there and, for a working example, it is not over-priced. It also offers a bit of interest in that the post is one of the more modern concrete types.

In order to enhance the Hornby signal cosmetically, you can start by getting rid of as much of the actual base as you can; as bought, it is 121mm high (30ft), which is bit much for an untapered post. Careful use of a coarse file is the best answer and reducing the base

LEFT AND OPPOSITE:
Hornby's stop signal does not really compare with the detailed Ratio post.

to almost nothing does help. You can also replace the operating wire with some slightly thinner florist's wire running through some small guides. However, you will still be stuck with that over-scale balance weight, since it serves as the operating lever.

The other improvements, which are largely cosmetic, include a complete repaint with matt enamels or acrylics, replacing the ladder with something much finer from the Ratio accessory pack, adding the safety hoops and ladder braces, and siting it close to the viewer and away from any scale posts.

There are sure to be modellers with some Hornby signals on their layout, as well as others who may have acquired them recently at a toy fair or car boot sale, who are happy to justify their inclusion. However, the amount of work required is without doubt disproportionate to the accuracy of the finished result.

RATIO SIGNALS

The whole Ratio range is of the highest quality and represents excellent value for money. Their 'advanced' kits contain sufficient components to construct four

signals, including multi-arm bracket versions, which work out at barely £2.00 per installation. They give great satisfaction once they are in place on a layout.

The kits can of course be constructed in full accordance with Ratio's instructions but that leaves the modeller with some head-scratching to do in an effort to find the right site for them. Rather, viewing them as an inexpensive 'builder's aid' will enable you to assemble the correct signal for (almost) any site. If they are that good and that versatile, why bother to do anything to them? The obvious answer is to make the very good into something even better.

The more expensive 'quick-assembly' LMS/BR(m) single-arm version comes with an excellent set of instructions backed by a useful summary of signalling in general. All the items in this part of the range include the components to make them operable by remote (thread/cable) levers. The kit is well designed and cleanly moulded, with nothing of significance that might warrant improvement. All that is needed is a paint job that does justice to the finished product. However, you do need to remember that this is

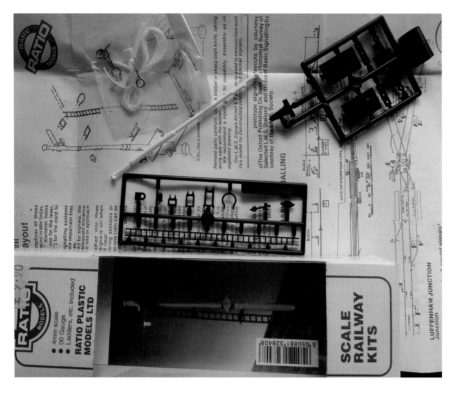

Ratio's working signals are a clever amalgamation of their excellent kit components with some very traditional 'string-n-spring' technology. Installation is best done as part of the baseboard construction as a retro-fit exercise would prove quite tricky.

intended as a working model and one that is reliant on small and fragile plastic parts. It does demand quite considerable patience and no little skill to get it operating smoothly and correctly, and even then it cannot be described as a robust item.

The range also includes two-arm versions, representing those frequent cases where box A's advanced starter shared the post with box B's distant. All the previous comments apply with particular emphasis on the need for care as one now has two independent working systems to get right.

ASSEMBLING THE RATIO MULTI-SIGNAL LNER KIT

Ratio has kits available for all the regions, but the LNER version is probably the most interesting challenge since it is probably the trickiest. The characteristic lattice posts are cleverly designed but do need some extra care in assembly. However, they do have the potential, with some small modifications, to transplant themselves to the opposite corner of the country and represent the very similar designs of the LSWR/BR(s). Indeed, even the

most cursory glance through the steam albums proves beyond doubt that these Southern variants outlasted their eastern and north-eastern counterparts by a good many years. They could be found all over Southern metals right through into the diesel period, and in several cases until the closure of the lines themselves.

Before examining this kit in detail, there are a few general observations that are worthy of mention. The single-post types can be worked on in the same way as the other kits in the range, except that these signals do not necessarily have to work. Select the appropriate kit for your company or BR region and just follow the instructions. You could and should add the important extra detail that your references suggest, and then just 'paint 'n plant', but you would be denying yourself the opportunity to exploit the true potential of these outstanding kits.

PREPARATION

If you have been diligent in your research you will probably have in mind several attractive prototypes, complete with their particular idiosyncrasies, that would look good on your layout.

Ratio's multi-signal kits are outstanding value, with sufficient parts to construct several quite complex posts. The LNER pack provides two attractive versions for the correct region and a splitting signal customized to LSWR/SR design.

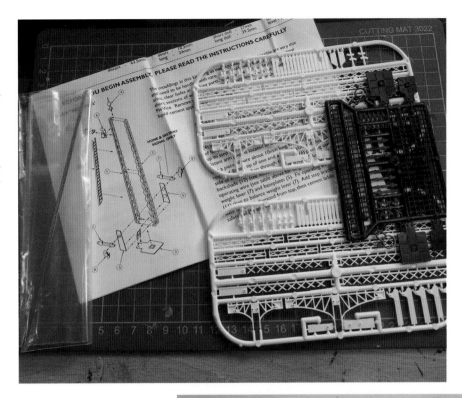

The kit contains two identical white plastic frets, flash-free and very crisply moulded, with enough parts for a variety of single-post and bracket signals. The third fret, in black plastic, has Ratio's usual mix of bases, ladders, balance weights and pivots. There are also several lengths of thin wire which can be used to make working models or merely to reproduce the operating wires on the prototype. (The wire is 0.47mm, which represents almost one and a half inches in this scale and is considerably thicker than the original. Thin florist's wire may be a better alternative, at 0.3mm.) The instructions cover two sides of A4 and include painting guides and simple exploded diagrams for the various assemblies.

This project will construct some types that are different from those illustrated, and where possible show the versatility of the kit and make maximum use of all the components, possibly augmented with some oddments from the bits box. This should yield a variety of both single-post and bracket signals carrying various combinations of arms. The manufacturer recommends that you paint the signal arms while they are still on the sprue; you can go a step further

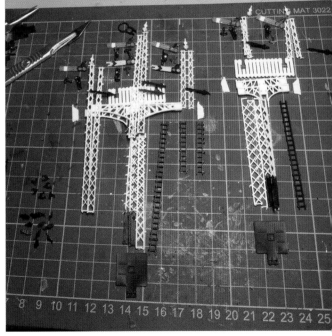

It is always best to paint as much as you can prior to assembly. The further the job progresses, the more intricate and delicate it becomes.

and paint any moving or non-glued parts at the same time. Do not forget that the fish-tail distant arms should be yellow and black, although this is not mentioned on the sheet. Once this has been done, at least for this project, all the components can be removed, using a new blade to ensure clean separation without damage to the often fragile items. In the normal modelling situation, it is of course best to cut each piece only as you need it for the signal you are building. Small bits are all too easy to misplace or lose to the legendary 'carpet fairies'!

When cutting these often quite delicate items, 'hacking' them off, using the scalpel at the most accessible spots and with minimum pressure, will hopefully avoid any damage or distortion. The moulding pips can then be trimmed away with the component properly supported on the cutting mat.

There is one final point to make concerning just how far you might want to go when reproducing a particular prototype signal. Generally, it is best to follow the same broad rules that apply to most scratch-building projects: what you leave out is as important as what you try to include. When studied in detail, signals are far more complicated than they may appear at first sight. This is par-ticularly true when looking at gantry and bracket types. Try to capture the essential character of the subject without becoming too embroiled in an attempt to replicate every component. This becomes even more critical if you are aiming for a working model. The more details you add, the more likely it is that they will interfere with or impede the moving parts.

MODIFICATIONS

If you are happy to accept one or all of the versions shown in the instructions, and can find appropriate sites for them on your layout, you can simply follow the given advice. However, if you are seeking something a bit more ambitious, which still fits into your plan, the following three examples will help to show what is possible:

1) A bracket 'splitting signal' suitable for a single-track branch as the 'home' ahead of a station giving access to a through line or platform, or diverting to a loop/platform via the secondary doll. (This is the arrangement referred to earlier at Harmans Cross and the model will be constructed to resemble that example.)

LEFT AND OPPOSITE ABOVE: *Harmans Cross down splitting home signals will be the basis for the SR version.*

2) A larger bracket 'splitting signal' that would be found in advance of a junction. The taller central doll protects the mainline; the slightly shorter right-hand doll indicates the junction and carries a 'fixed-distant' warning of a station/hazard ahead; the third short doll to the left could give access to a loop/sidings/platform or relief line.

3) A short, single-post 'starter' with a supplementary or calling-on arm; while this is a quite typical platform-end feature in real life, this one is merely designed to make use of the spare components from the two previous examples. To add further interest, the post also features a 'cash register', which would show the route authorized by the arm.

The actual assemblies are quite straightforward, apart from the need to design and plan the various components into their new configurations. This will

This Southern starter will be used as the inspiration to produce an LNER model.

also reveal the need for some extra items to supplement those included in the kit. First, and most important, is the 0.50mm rod that will form the vital safety rails and other ironwork. It is also helpful if you can find some spare work platforms and other details. For example, you might want to seek out some LSWR finials appropriate for the Harmans Cross version, but choose to stick with those supplied for the others.

MINOR ERRORS

To be honest, and despite its obviously attractive appearance, the kit will not deliver a 'typical' LNER/BR(E or NE) signal. All the many independent railways that made up this major region had their own designs, as did the post-grouping LNER itself. However, by the 1950s, finials were as rare as the lattice posts and those that did remain were usually quite different from the rather GWR style in the box. There are more suitable white-metal examples available from specialist suppliers and it is a matter of personal choice just how far you wish to go in search of authenticity.

One other point concerns the balance weights. The kits always show these at the base of the posts, where they can also be used as operating levers. In prototype reality, however, this is simply wrong. The

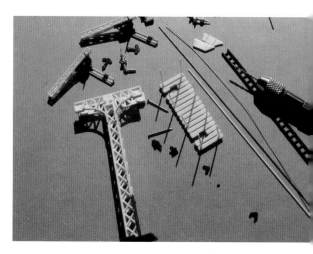

It is advisable to do all the drilling and fixing for the safety rails and pivot pins before assembling the brackets.

images all show them to be mounted relatively close to their respective arm and always projecting on the same side. Unless you are one of the minority trying to make working signals, this more accurate appearance is the better option.

With regard to the safety rails, it is wise to drill the platforms and fix the uprights before assembly. Also, carefully carve and scrape the provided safety hoops to a more realistic thinner and rounded profile, as they are far too heavy as supplied.

Assembling the cleverly designed lattice posts can prove to be somewhat difficult as the components are extremely light. Align the segments against a reasonably heavy straight-edge and carefully apply small quantities of liquid-poly. Once the job is reasonably secure the post can be lifted and made satisfactorily robust with more poly.

LNER TO LSWR

The following is not a solution that would satisfy the purist and there are other routes to obtaining 100 per cent accurate LSWR/SR/BR(S) signals, but all of these require considerable skill with the soldering iron and an equal level of dexterity when it comes to some very small and delicate brass components. Nonetheless, the end result of this bit of kit conversion does produce a visually acceptable alternative and is easy and economical.

Very little work is actually required. The key points are to fit new finials (white-metal castings from Springside), to fabricate and fit the different styles of balance weights, and finally to paint the normally black ironwork in the soft grey favoured by the LSWR and often continued into SR and BR(S) days. However, while this will yield a perfectly acceptable result, it is worth going the extra mile and producing a replica of an actual signal, copied from a suitable image or personal photograph or research. You will also need a scrap of ultra-thin (ten-thou/0.27mm) plasticard for the sighting board; you can also cut a sliver from this to represent the plank wired to the base of the ladder.

For part of this exercise the selected prototype was the 'up' bracket signal controlling the access to

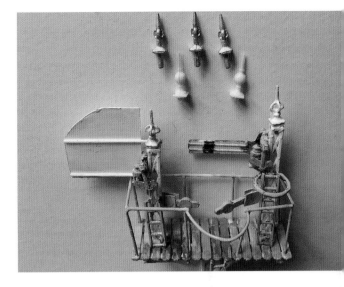

The finials in the kit seem closer to the GWR than the intended LNER. This is the completed Southern bracket fitted with Springside LSWR finials, with the original and the more correct NER versions shown for comparison.

Harmans Cross station on the Swanage Railway. This will not be featured in any of the period albums as, like the station itself, it is a preservation-era installation. However, it is always worth a trip for field research and photography!

The three signals ready for installation; note the additional steelwork and the balance weights located to match the prototypes. They represent outstanding value, given the modest price of the kit, providing a few hours of enjoyable work for a nice result.

WHETHER TO WEATHER?

There is one final aspect that is rarely (if ever) covered in articles in the model press or in modelling guides, and that is the role of 'weathering' in respect of signals. This is somewhat strange since the humble signal was surely exposed to more weather than almost every other railway artefact. It does seem that most modellers (including myself) are inclined, however, to leave their signals astonishingly and improbably pristine.

In the real world of the steam-era railway, the regular maintenance of signals was of course an essential for the staff of the S & T departments. However, maintenance did not necessarily imply much in the way of repaints. Worn, rotten or rusted items were quickly replaced and the offending components either left for scrap or recovered for recycling. This in itself gives an original excuse for some extra character cameos; how about raiding the bits box for spare posts, dolls, arms or ladders and leaving them at the lineside to moulder away or await disposal?

As for your installed signals, upon which you have just lavished such care, the weathering should be fairly discreet, refer to images of the Harmans Cross bracket signal, which do show the subtle effects of neglect. The work should amount to little more than a general dulling of the paintwork and some rust on the metal areas. Pastel dust is probably the best medium, with perhaps just the odd touch of rust-coloured enamel for the worst-affected areas. Less is more should always be the rule.

The Southern splitting signal halts the westbound progress of this 'bashed' S15 in front of the Superquick box.

The LNER junction signal and Wills LNER box clear V2 Durham Light Infantry from main to branch. The branch doll also carries a fixed distant, indicating some permanent restriction ahead.

The small starting signal has been further embellished with a cash-register indicator and calling-on arm; it looks quite happy here, even if it is rather far from its intended region.

CONCLUSIONS

Whichever company or region you choose, it is pretty certain that the Ratio range will have the individual signal or kit(s) to meet your needs. They have certainly proved their worth on many hundreds, if not thousands, of layouts, from humble branch lines to massive and complex mainline efforts. Their quality and accuracy are excellent, especially in view of their relatively low price-tag. Above all, they are exceptionally versatile and can be modified and combined to reproduce a realistic miniature of even the most grandiose or bizarre prototype.

Over the years, 'Wessex Lines' has sprouted no fewer than forty-four posts and brackets carrying ninety arms, to which East Ilsley now adds a further nine posts and twenty arms. And that is not counting the ground signals! Almost every single one of these is based either on a known real-life example or, failing that, uses best practice to fit its given functions. Some do feature some scratch-built additions to the existing Ratio components.

CUSTOMIZING AND DETAILING SIGNALS

The following section is as much about inspiration as it is about information. The images of 'Wessex Lines' show the immense variety of signals that can be made from the contents of Ratio's LNER and GWR kits. Hopefully, the 'whistle-stop tour may get you thinking about improving or even replacing some of your own signals.

SPECTACLES AND GLAZING

Many modellers seem to struggle with (or choose to ignore) achieving a realistic appearance for the 'glass' spectacles on the signals. The most obvious answer is to use enamel paint on the Ratio plastic mouldings, but this may not always produce a very realistic solution. The use of matt green and red looks quite wrong for polished glass. Equally, using gloss or even satin greens and reds still just makes them look 'painted'. You can just settle for one or the other and live with the result; indeed, if you are modelling upper-quadrant signals, with their relatively small spectacles, this is more or less acceptable. However, if your layout features the elegant GWR tapered-post wooden signals, a more sophisticated approach is required, as the spectacles are just too big to be ignored.

After trying many different ideas, it seems that the most effective is to carefully and completely scalpel out both spectacles and replace them with very thin plastiglaze, pre-painted with Humbrol stained-glass red and turquoise. It is an extreme solution, and tricky to the point of being detrimental to your eyesight and sanity, but if you can get it right, it is spot on!

The bracket down starter at Crowcombe on the ever-popular West Somerset Railway; the bracket would help to give a clear view for through services otherwise obscured by an ancient conifer!

More bracket signals, this time courtesy of Ratio's GWR wood post kit; on the left is the down home, and to the right is the up starter for Torpoint station.

When it came to the signalling on 'Wessex Lines' and later on 'East Ilsley', with literally dozens of GWR and LSWR arms to consider, something quicker and definitely easier was needed. It came in the form of combining those two enamel versions. Each spectacle received a carefully applied gloss 'undercoat' of red and duck-egg green, followed by several coats of the aforementioned stained-glass red and turquoise. It may not be the perfect answer, but it is easy and relatively quick, and a distinct improvement over the alternatives.

There is one other idea that might be worth passing on to those modellers with only a few signals to worry about. Salvage some scraps from Christmas decorations, the cheaper and thinner the better. Select some suitable red and turquoise pieces and glue them (using liquid-poly) behind the carved-out spectacles, then carefully trim them to shape. It is not a rush job but the end result is not half bad.

Why is it 'turquoise' and not plain 'green'? The answer is that the actual spectacle glasses are turquoise, which then shows as green when they are illuminated by their oil lamps. To witness the effect, visit your nearest preserved railway on a winter afternoon and judge for yourself as evening draws in.

Another shot of Crowcombe's down starter, showing that the 'green' spectacle is in fact turquoise.

ADDING EXTRA DETAIL

- **Safety rails:** safety rails are an absolute must, even on comparatively short posts. The very least that you need is the simple 'hoop' at the top of the ladder. These are provided with some of the kits but are, sadly, often the wrong shape and too coarse or bulky. You can spend some time trying to file or carve these into something with a more realistic profile, but it is better and probably quicker to fabricate replacements from plastic strip or rod, depending on your prototype. Be careful to get the shape and position correct since different companies used their own designs. Always work to a photograph of your chosen signal.
- **Ladders:** the steel ladders on the prototype were relatively slender affairs and will prove to be somewhat fragile on the model. They certainly needed to be braced to the post at regular intervals. This can be replicated with plastic rod, for both accuracy and added strength.
- **Circuiting:** by the time signalling had matured in the steam era, much of the track had received electrical circuiting. This showed up on the signalbox diagram to indicate the presence or passage of a train. Where this was not in place there would be a small telephone box attached to the post. If a train was held at the signal for any length of time, it was the fireman's duty to phone the box and remind the signalman of their existence. Your 'home' or 'stop' signal posts should therefore carry either a small diamond-shaped plate, to indicate track-circuiting, or the small phone cabinet. However, under the wonderful catch-all heading of 'a prototype for everything', there are plenty of examples where both exist on the same post.
- **Deterrents:** in many instances, signals are located on station platforms, where their ladders are obviously an irresistible temptation for 'spotters and photters'. The answer from officialdom was to wire a heavy plank of wood to the lower rungs – another nice piece of very simple modelling which adds character and authenticity.
- **Guy ropes:** most, if not all, tall signals needed to be braced by steel guy ropes. In the case of the bigger bracket or gantry signals, which could be carrying a large number of arms, there would be a very real need for several such wires. In some instances, these might well run right across the tracks, from one side of a cutting to the other. It is obviously a feature well worth the effort to model, using nylon threads and track pins, but with a word of warning. Plastic kit-built signals are already quite delicate items and hence are very prone to damage, especially during track-cleaning is in progress. They can also be difficult to install in an absolutely upright position. Guy ropes, however commendable, only

Rarely modelled but quite frequently encountered, these illuminated speed-restriction signs would be seen anywhere where a permanent speed limit was in force. The locations might include stations, mainline junctions, viaducts or similar places where the engineers required them.

These tall Southern posts (inspired by examples on the old Somerset & Dorset) were necessary to ensure that sight-lines were clear, despite the adjacent cuttings, curves and bridge work. The up home and distant carries low-level repeating arms to be seen through the arch.

Common-or-garden GWR 'stop' signals at a point on 'Wessex Lines' where the outer and inner routes come close together. On the left the tall signal is Stoneycombe's outer home, the short post is the up advanced starter and on the right is the outer home for Torpoint on the coast line. (Each signal actually protects an 'electric block' with its own supply. To run trains all around the circuit requires each consecutive block to be energized and its switch thrown.)

These graceful bracket signals are the up main and loop starters at the principal station. The repeaters at the lower level make sighting easier for crews using the full length of the island platform.

The bracket signal at Tunnel Junction, on the route from the coast, carries the down starters and distants for the complex point-work ahead. The left-hand pair take the trains back round to Sherborne as services on the up-controller, while the right-hand pair enable it to continue through the tunnel to Stoneycombe and Dainton on the down-main. (The system works and allows complete trains to be reversed from down to up workings, and vice versa.) The signal is on a rail-built post and was inspired by an SECR installation hurriedly sketched while on a business trip.

exacerbate these problems. The best advice is to try it and see how it goes.

- **Bases:** signal kits always include bases. These are useful aids to handling during construction, and to maintaining the post upright during installation, but they are most definitely non-prototypical. Signal posts should be planted in the ground and not standing on top of it. To disguise the base, conceal it with ballast or 'grass', depending on the site. If the signal is on a platform you can get away with the base, but do check your references for real-world images.

- **Balance weights:** balance weights, which are used to ensure that the signal arm always returns to the 'stop' position, are rather contentious when it comes to kit builds. The fact they are provided on the sprue does not necessarily mean that they must be used. In fact, the reverse is equally likely. They are usually found on the signals furthest from the box, where the added weight and drag of several hundred yards of wire can cause the signal at best to be sluggish and at worst to remain stubbornly 'off'. Check the prototype and also be prepared, if you need them at all, to make your own versions in line with the real ones. Kit versions can sometimes be inappropriately large and heavy.

- **Operating mechanisms:** another area for potential detailing is the actual operating mechanism for the signal arms. The kits will almost certainly include the many small guides and brackets; they may also include a coil of ultra-thin plastic 'wire'. However, while it easy to fix the various brackets in their correct positions, it is far from easy to straighten that coil and prevent it from bowing when you try to secure it. Frankly, you might prefer to leave it off than have the struggle! The thinnest florist's wire, nipped to the correct lengths, will do the job, but you may feel it is too shiny to be convincing. The only other alternative is to use nylon thread fixed with tiny amounts of superglue.

- **Sighting boards:** you will see on many of the prototype photos that the signal arms are backed by a quarter-circle of white-painted metal. This is common device to help the arm to stand-out from a cluttered or over-bright background. It is an easy

The down inner homes for Sherborne: (right to left) down-main, loop and goods-loop.

No busy station should be without a gantry and this one carries Sherborne's down starters; the small bracket signal with its cash-register governs the loco spur for the station pilot.

In real life, the original Signal & Telegraph engineers were often faced with a lack of space for essential signalling. Here they have made use of the shed roof to site Knighton's up starters.

feature to model from some thin plasticard and is another way of adding character to your installation. The same purpose can also be represented by a whitewashed panel on a bridge when there is a signal located in front of it.

SOME BASIC 'RULES'

It is always worth remembering a few basic rules:

- Always model signals that are appropriate to the tasks they are expected to carry out on your layout; familiarize yourself with correct railway practice.

- Site the signals so that they make their best visual contribution to the scene, but make sure your miniature enginemen could see them in good time.
- Add as much detail and character as you can. Where possible, re-create actual prototypes.
- Take care to keep the posts vertical from every aspect and do not forget how delicate and fragile they really are. Plastic kits are easier to build than to repair.
- Judge for yourself how close together you can place your signals. Much will depend upon the actual shape of your track plan and the presence of any

Knighton's signalling from the other side of the bridges. The view looks down the snow-clad length of Winterbourne bank and shows the back of the bracket post carrying the down home arms.

The crew of the little 'C'-class take it easy as they trundle off the bridge with a short freight past Torpoint's up inner home signal. The down starter is also 'off' at the end of the long curved platform.

'masking features' like bridges, cuttings, curves and trees or buildings may enable you to minimize the distance. (Your ever-reliable Mk I eye-ball will tell what works and what does not.)

- It is worth considering the option of making your signals removable for track-cleaning. It will depend upon the nature of your baseboard; the general principle is to drill, insert and secure a longish steel pin or small nail into the bottom of the post, which then fits into a locating hole on the layout. Make sure that both holes are vertical!

- The hobby as a whole is much driven by pure nostalgia and there is a great deal of satisfaction in re-creating your own version of a once familiar location.

ABOVE LEFT AND RIGHT: *Two examples of Southern-style ground signals at Sherborne, both from a pack of well-detailed white-metal castings.*

There are several GWR ground signals in the appropriate Ratio packs. At the last count, there are more than twenty to be found on 'Wessex Lines'.

ABOVE LEFT AND RIGHT: *These illuminated 'stop' signs – elderly white-metal castings of unknown ancestry – were relatively common in sheds and yards, protecting dead-end roads or mandatory danger points such as access roads or turntables. The ground-mounted calling-on arm is a less common feature.*

Salisbury's Tunnel Junction, scratch-built from photographs, is all about nostalgia. It has been lovingly re-created in an appropriate setting as Axemouth Tunnel Junction on 'Wessex Lines', with the allotments and the familiar cottages (from Bilteezi) squeezed in.

CHAPTER NINE

POINT-RODDING, SIGNAL WIRES AND LEVEL-CROSSINGS

INTRODUCTION

DO YOU NEED RODDING AND WIRES?

The honest answer is 'yes'…and 'no'! If your objective is produce a layout that is as close as you can get to being a miniature version of the real thing, then your signal box must at least appear to be connected to the points and signals under its control. You must reproduce what exists on the prototype, and especially so when this includes details that are readily apparent even to the casual observer. Against that criteria, the rodding and wires become a 'must'.

If, however, your aspirations are more modest in terms of the exact degree of authenticity you hope to achieve, you can probably get away without them. In fact, on a large or larger layout, leaving them off could become almost a necessity rather than an omission. A big layout usually has more movement and more to see. From a purely practical standpoint, this means more track to be cleaned more often. In this case, a maze of point-rodding and extensive runs of signal wires will get in the way and will also be vulnerable to damage. It is equally certain that neither the operator nor the visitor will be likely to notice their absence.

ABOVE LEFT AND RIGHT: *With platform-mounted signal boxes, the point-rodding and signal wires are fed beneath the surface to emerge from a cavity in the platform face. These are at Crowcombe and Williton on the West Somerset Railway.*

RECENT DEVELOPMENTS

For many years, even the most detailed layouts lacked the necessary connections between the signal box and its associated points and signals. To be fair, their absence was not that likely to be noticed and they were much less of an essential than most other details. In addition, were no available kits and a similar lack of readily accessible prototype information. Those modellers who were prepared to go the extra mile in pursuit of perfection almost invariably added such items when everything else had been completed. They became a finishing touch, to lift the layout to a higher plane.

It is not strictly true that there were 'no kits'. In fact, there were no specifically produced accessory packs, but some of key components had long been included in certain kits. The comprehensive white-metal 'Signal Box Interior' kit from Springside, had a few point-rodding cranks and some signal-wire pulleys – just enough to model some of the fittings nearest to the box – and there were also some useful tips on how best to install these components. It was not much, but it was a start and many modellers doubtless made good use of them.

The Springside kit is still available and Wills Scenics have recently introduced two kits, one specifically with all the complex cranks and joints needed for an authentic installation, and a second that is a simple supporting pack of additional point-rodding for longer runs. These are currently priced at £10 and £8 respectively. As with all Wills kits, there are clear instructions on the often tricky assembly of so many small pieces (although there is no master illustration showing how the various sub-assemblies connect to the runs of rodding, which would be useful). PECO, who currently market the Wills range and publish Railway Modeller, were quick off the mark with two well-detailed features in their June and July 2015 issues. These have proved to be essential reading for anyone embarking on the task.

Although recent developments and the provision of kits have solved some of the problems, it is not quite as straightforward as simply rushing out and buying a kit. The instructions and the arti-

ABOVE: *The rodding and wires follow the same paths wherever possible; their routes are a compromise between ease of access for the S&T engineers and protection of public rights of way.*

The Wills Scenics kit for point-rodding is very well moulded and usually free of flash. The items are very small and it is important, for good fixing, to carefully remove any moulding pips and to ensure that the ends of the rods are absolutely square. The long-serving white-metal castings of essential guide wheels for signal wires and cranks for point-rodding are from Springside.

cles both describe the correct installations done at the appropriate time, which is of course during the initial track-laying. Needless to say, the rodding should pass beneath the rails and between the sleepers, and the actual crank mountings should then be embedded in the ballast. That is as it should be, but it is not much help if you want to install these devices retrospectively into a fully complete and operating layout. In most cases, this means trying to thread delicate plastic components beneath track-work that is firmly secured to the baseboards with a hefty dose of good old 'PVA mix'. There are probably far more modellers with completed layouts than there are with new-builds or drastic rebuilds, so this is potentially quite problematic.

The big question is, can these beautifully crafted precision items be successfully retro-fitted to an existing layout? The best way to find out was to pick a suitable site on 'Wessex Lines' and explore what might be achieved. The signal box at Knighton Yard was ideal for the exercise, since it overlooks multiple tracks and has some fairly complex point-work to operate.

RETRO-FITTING POINT-RODDING

The first step is to draw the existing track plan in as large a scale as possible, perhaps on a sheet of A2 drawing paper. Plot the optimum routes from the box to all the designated points. Try to keep the runs of rodding as close together as much as you can and, where possible, group the cranks in one place. This is not just for neatness, but it is the correct prototype approach to simplify the job of the S & T engineers. From the plan you should be able to make an initial count of the numbers of each component that you will need and also get an approximate idea for the amount of rodding to tie the whole scheme together. Do not take chances. Re-visit the layout and, with some spare bits of plastic, balsa strip or even string, test your plans in the real world and amend them as necessary. Remember that you will ultimately have to excavate and burrow your way beneath a great many tracks, including some major running-lines. There is an ever-present risk of 'collateral damage' and this must somehow be kept to an absolute minimum.

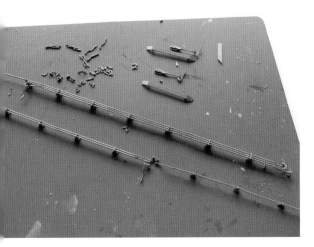

Two runs of rodding assembled on the work-bench and ready for installation at Knighton Yard on 'Wessex Lines'. The assembly of the cranks is more or less according to the artwork, but their various joins to the actual rodding are the result of experimentation. The interlocking mechanisms have been cut short to avoid any attempt to thread the linkage beneath the rails.

The rodding run on the approach to Knighton. The outer run should extend for a further 18in to the facing point on the down main; the two inner runs are some 12in short of where they should cross beneath the 'down' to operate the double-slip on the 'up', which gives access to the loops and yard. That would require most of a second kit.

Once you are happy that your final planned routes are both realistic and achievable, you can re-calculate your total requirements and their attendant costs. For 'Wessex Lines', this involved a sharp intake of breath followed by a long silence. Completing the plan would require a minimum of three kits and five support packs, a total outlay of £70 just to cover a six-foot stretch of the mainline. Extending the exercise across the whole of 'Wessex Lines' would involve a budget that ran into hundreds of pounds, not to mention the many hours of digging out ballast and assembling kits, and then all the painting and making good.

Wills have produced a beautifully made and highly accurate little kit. It is no doubt ideal, as long as it is installed as part of the initial track-laying, as recommended on the instructions. However, the components are small and quite tricky to cut out and assemble, so fitting them retrospectively to an established layout is a near impossibility, unless you are prepared to accept a very high degree of compromise. The principal difficulties are in the threading of the rods, at a constant right-angle, beneath several

Emerging from the down side of the box, and minus the required third rodding, this run is still between 24in and 30in short of its objective. The crank is there purely for effect; fitting the adjusters further up and to all three rods would compensate for the distance from the box to the cross-overs at the far end of the loops. Note the various guide wheels for the signal wires, including those that would carry the wires across to the yard signals.

The various rods and wires, as they emerge from the locking room; when it comes to adding the walkway this will be made sufficiently wide to partially cover these items, disguising the fact that they have no inward linkage.

The protective covers over the very delicate interlocking mechanisms obviously conceal them from view. It is a simple task to make your own versions from thin plastic sheet. Adding a bit of micro-rod for the linkage should give the impression that all the appropriate points are interlocked. It is just an hour's work and at a cost of a few pence!

tracks using the small gap between the sleepers and the even smaller gap between the ballast and the underside of the rails, and the essential changes in height and direction at either end. It is expensive in terms of the rodding and cranks and, with a wide baseboard, can also take its toll on the back!

It took over five hours to assemble the two runs illustrated, and that was done at the work-bench in a good light. A further two hours were needed to install them; and three-quarters of the main running-lines, never mind the loops and yard, still needed attention. The cost/benefit analysis just does not add up, especially when a feature may have been acceptable for many years and no one has ever commented on the omission. As always, it is down to each individual modeller to decide whether to invest the time and money to retro-fit this element, or whether to 'fudge' the issue with some suitably sized plastic strip or micro-rod.

There is one additional point of detail, particularly for those countless modellers who focus on the GWR/BR(W) layouts. If you are really committed to absolute accuracy, you will know that the company's point-rodding was actually round in profile; that in the kits represents the later square-section BR version. There is also a general understanding that the GWR rodding was painted red, although the few colour images of the period yield little discernible evidence of this.

Finally, regardless of whether you intend to use the kits or to take the DIY approach, you can always limit your runs to those nearest the signal box or those closest to the viewer. Elsewhere, especially in goods yards, shed yards and on branch lines, the humble point levers did the job on the real railway and they can do it on your layout too.

ABOVE, ALL IMAGES: *A typical row of levers beside a run of points at Knighton yards and a suitably posed shunting scene. The simplest, but not necessarily the easiest, way of moving heavy point mechanisms is by hand-operated levers. They are quite common features in wayside goods yards and on branch lines. They are also encountered in marshalling yards and loco depots where movements are best and most quickly authorized on the spot by the appropriate staff.*

SIGNAL WIRES

RE-CREATING SIGNAL WIRES

For those who 'spotted' in the days of the once-ubiquitous semaphore signal, there was nothing more exciting than the sound of the signal wires twitching as they ran beneath the edge of the platform. Even on a relatively humble wayside station, it would mean that something was due any minute. What might it be? At Challow, it meant gazing to the east to see which of the 'down-pegs' had dropped – a goods or stopper on the relief, a semi-fast coming into the platform from the main? Maybe both through arms were off, in which case the eyes were peeled and the pencils poised, awaiting a possible 'cop' on an express.

Sadly, you can no more re-create the sound of the wires on your layout than you can relive the eager anticipation of not knowing what was due. However, you can at least make a stab at reproducing the wires themselves; in comparison with the tasks associated with the point-rodding, it is relatively easy. There are only two components involved: the wires and small 'posts' that carried them.

In respect of the real railway these are quite small and inconspicuous features, so much so that they are hard to spot in most photographs. It is not surprising, then, that they are even harder to find on most layouts. Equally, there seems to be little in the way of any standard design to the posts and they receive scant coverage even in the most detailed of reference books (apart from a few that are too complicated to attempt in 1/76th scale). The posts themselves seemed to be of basic angle-iron but with small banks of roller guides attached to the back; each of those individual guides carried just one wire. These could certainly be re-created in miniature, but would the end result justify the time and effort? To some extent this is still good news for modellers since, lacking a definitive and viable prototype, you are free to design your own versions, which now only have to satisfy a few basic criteria: they need to be quick and cheap to make, easy to install and still pretty much damage-proof; and they have to support the requisite number of wires.

Two examples of wire runs on 'Wessex Lines'. Nylon threads pass freely through small holes in 'I'- or 'L'-shaped plastic strips, which are then planted outside the cess, before the threads are tightened and secured.

After a fair bit of trial and error, the best solution on 'Wessex Lines' proved to be one or other of the plastic strips from Greenscenes – in some cases, the very smallest 'L' sections and in others the smallest 'I' sections. They are both perhaps a little on the chunky side but, despite being sited unavoidably close to the running-lines, it does mean that they are slightly less prone to collateral damage during heavy-duty track-cleaning.

The wires are simply nylon thread, fed through small pre-drilled holes in the posts. This method enables them to be pulled taut, even over comparatively long runs, and is simply a ground-level mini version of the way barbed-wire fencing is constructed on rural layouts.

It is a rather fiddly exercise for what is no more than a bit of extra window-dressing, and no layout could be considered to be incomplete without them, but they do overcome that sense of signals standing in splendid isolation from their controlling box. The choice is yours but, if you want to try it, here are a few tips with some supporting illustrations.

INSTALLING SIGNAL WIRES: PREPARATION

The following sequence is just one way of installing signal wires – you may well find an alternative that better suits your layout, your skills, and possibly your patience! The wires should emerge from beneath the front of your signal box and run along that same side of the track, with one wire to every arm that it operates.

1) Select your choice of post ('L'- or 'I'-section plastic strip) and cut into short lengths of approximately 20mm. That will allow you to have a post 12mm (3 scale-feet) above ground and still leave enough at the base for it to be securely planted into your baseboard.

2) Count the number of arms that apply on your layout, unless you have a busy multi-track mainline junction, it will probably be no more than four or five in each direction. Starting at the top of each small post, use one of your smallest drills (perhaps 0.05mm) to make the necessary holes to accept the wires.

Signal wires running at ground level close to the box before being carried on short steel posts out towards the signals. Wires cannot perform sharp angles so each major change of direction requires a pulley wheel.

3) The number of posts that you need is determined by the actual distance to your furthest signal, with the posts planned at roughly 240mm intervals (60 scale-feet). The number of holes needed in each post decreases by one every time you reach an intermediate signal, or you can simply drill the lot and ignore an increasing number when threading the wires out from the box.

4) There are various ways to thread the posts, depending on the keenness of your eye and the steadiness of your hand. If you are 20/20 in both those assets, loose-threading (A) is the quickest. If you are less confident, a simple jig (B) may make life easier.

(The descriptions apply to wires on the far side of the track running to the right, as viewed from the signal box; the principles apply equally to any run.)

CREATING A RUN IN SITU (A)

1) Starting at the signal-box end (left) of the run, cut the first wire/thread slightly over-length and thread it through the top hole. Leave enough for the final positioning around the guide wheels and beneath the box. Secure it with a small touch of superglue. Thread the remaining posts on to that wire but do not secure them yet.

2) Repeat this with each wire in turn until your mini fence is complete and ready for installation.

3) Slide the posts along the wires, 'planting' them at their predetermined intervals. Strictly speaking, every time your supporting posts are opposite a signal post, there should be another guide wheel to carry the wire(s) to the base – one for each arm. This can be quite a complex mini-installation if the signal post is a 'splitter', controlling a junction and loops with its numerous arms. If the run is on the far side of the baseboard, it may possible to 'fudge' some of the intricacies and still convince the eye.

4) Where signal posts are sited on the opposite side of the track it is as well to study some prototype images to see how this was done and how, if at all, the wire(s) are protected. Or, take the day off and see how it is done on your favourite preserved line.

5) When each thread reaches its outermost post, draw it taut with tweezers and secure it with a small dab of superglue.

CREATING A RUN OFF SITE (B)

1) First, make a small jig, from a suitable piece of decent wood into which you drill a series of small holes (to accept your posts as 'push-fit') at roughly 3in (80mm) spacings. Plant your posts in the holes, ensuring that they all face the same way. It does not matter whether you prefer to thread left to right or vice versa, as long as you have those short spare lengths on the left after gluing them to that first post.

2) Proceed as above, working under a good light and threading each wire through all the posts using needle-point tweezers. It is easier to thread everything through everything with all the wires going the full distance to the outermost post.

A simple jig for assembling wire-runs off-site and equally handy for threading post-and-wire fences. It's just a smooth 24" piece of 'two-by-one' (50mm x 25mm if you prefer!) with a series of pre-drilled holes at various intervals, but it works.

3) When complete, carefully lay the whole the length on the layout and slide each post to roughly its final position.

4) Using a smallish drill, bradawl or similar tool, make the holes in the baseboard at the correct distances ready to accept the posts. Keep the holes neatly in line and outside the cess (the cinder pathway between the edge of the ballast and the verge).

5) Plant and glue the first post and then carefully adjust the remainder to their planting holes, gluing each post as you go. Be careful not to let the assembly twist or become tangled, and continue to refrain from securing the wires.

6) Carry on until all the posts are planted and firmly glued in place. The last one should be directly beside your furthest signal(s). From this point, the exercise is the same as in the previous example.

7) Finally, draw all the spare lengths together and glue them at close intervals beneath the protec-

tive footboards at the base of the box. This gives the correct appearance as if they were worked by the actual levers.

8) If you have used one of the kits discussed in the section on point-rodding, you will have the small flat wheels ready for the purpose for which they were intended. Site them immediately in front of the footboards so that your wires can be properly guided around the right-angle between the box and their route beside the track.

9) Painting is relatively easy – just a thin coat of metallic black for the wires and matt black for the posts; for contrast, the posts could be done with a pale grey to represent galvanized metal.

CROSSING TRACKS

There are obviously innumerable occasions when a box is responsible for signals situated on the opposite side of the running-lines. This can mean passing beneath the single track of a branch line or threading under perhaps six or more tracks at a busy station or mainline junction. The modeller has two alternatives in this sort of situation. The easiest to explain and to install is simply to lay another wire run, this time from right to left, but still on the same side as the box. Take the posts out to a site directly opposite the furthest signal and, using exactly the same principles as before, take the top wire down to a pulley wheel so that it can turn through the right-angle and appear to cross beneath the tracks. Work back towards the box, adding a pulley or set of pulleys in line with the signals opposite. Snip away the spare lengths, and paint to complete the exercise.

The alternative is to create a complete new wire run on the far side of the tracks and take all the wires from the box straight across in one go. This means that the pulleys will now be needed on that far side and not immediately below the box. It is then an exact repeat of the original operations.

POINTS TO REMEMBER

• Installing signal wires is a relatively straightforward business and can be carried out at any time. It can be done as the layout is being built or installed as a

sort of afterthought on a fully completed and operating railway, providing you have left sufficient space.

• The only significant costs are the small pulley wheels and even those are pence not pounds. If you cannot source these little items you might get away with using the female half of a small 'popper'; it may not be 100 per cent accurate, but you will score top marks for ingenuity and economics!

• It demands little in the way of tools or skills; but it does require a degree of care, a sharp eye, a steady hand and some patience.

• Remember that there must be a wire for every signal arm and that also includes any ground signals. (It may be better to restrict the exercise to a few more obvious locations. 'Wessex Lines' has eleven boxes controlling ninety arms on forty-four posts – needless to say, they are not all 'wired'!)

• If the wire runs need to extend through stations, as is often the case, simply cut the spare bottom portion from the posts and glue the wire-carrying section to the face of the platforms.

• Where the wires have to cross the cess and appear to burrow beneath the track(s), you can replicate this by placing small-diameter tube or half-tube, partly buried in the cinders and ballast, and running to or from the pulley wheel to the signal post. Paint the sections in some dull reddish colour to represent lengths of pipe. (If the wires coincide with point-rodding, then you can imply that they all lie beneath any planked walkways that may be in place).

LEVEL-CROSSINGS

BACKGROUND

It may be a generalization, but level-crossings are probably more popular with modellers than they ever were with the real railways. A level-crossing is such an attractive feature to reproduce and can add welcome interest to even the blandest stretch of track. It does not seem to matter whether it is actually a working model or simply a scenic accessory; it is just a basic must-have.

Like most features on Britain's systems, level-crossings exist in an infinitely variable array of designs

This image shows how roadways maintain their level and metalled surface before, through and beyond the actual crossing. Ramps and boarded crossings would be found only in station areas or farm crossings and these were rare. The superb thirty-two-doll telephone pole is commonplace by the real railway but rarely modelled. AUSTIN ATTEWELL

A metalled road surface as seen from inside the crossing. AUSTIN ATTEWELL

and sizes. They range from a simple pair of rather rickety gates on some meandering rural branch line, operated by the train crew, to the major affairs that caused so much irritation in town centres such as Gloucester and Exeter. The actual constructions themselves were equally different and each company or contractor had their own ideas as to how these somewhat basic facilities should look and work. It would seem that, even on a simple branch line, no two were identical, even if only because they had to cope with the different needs of various roads.

KITS

The demands of the road layout – whether it is a busy main road or a by-way or lane that provides access to another part of the station yard – must be borne in mind when contemplating a crossing on your layout. The main road will need something much more adaptable and controlled than the by-way, for example. The key point to remember is that all railway/public highway crossings must be protected by gates and these must be controlled automatically, or by a traditional signal box or crossing keeper, and must be kept properly locked.

There are currently three usable kits available this side of scratch-building, of which two are near identical in appearance and purpose (although they do vary in price). The third is the smallest and hence the cheapest, but it may turn out to offer some unique benefits. (There is a fourth kit – for a simple pair of gates designed for an 'accommodation crossing' for farm traffic – as well as a ready-to-site version, from Bachmann 'Scenecraft', which, with its current price of nearly £40, is a costly way of solving a very simple problem.)

Fortunately, the scratch-build route is easy to research and the construction is not too taxing. Most albums will include one or more images while the books on signalling will provide technical details

Two level-crossing kits ready for assembly – the Airfix/Dapol model from the 1960s alongside the twenty-first-century version by Gaugemaster. How many modellers ever use those improbable ramps and in-fills?

as well as drawings and photographs. There are also plenty of resources online; simply search under 'steam-era gated level-crossings UK'.

ASSEMBLING THE LEVEL-CROSSING KITS

The two main level-crossing kits are very similar in concept, but they certainly differ in age. The one currently produced by Dapol, under its resurrected 'Kitmaster' branding, is the old, familiar Airfix crossing that is now about fifty years old and has never really been out circulation. Its newer rival comes from Gaugemaster, part of their Fordhampton range and manufactured for them by Faller. It has been on the market for only a year or so and seems to be aimed at the same beginners-upwards audience as the original 'Airfix-at-Woolies' version. They are equally easy to obtain, but, while the Dapol is still only £6.50, the Gaugemaster is £11.50, and most if not all model shops will have them on the shelf. The cheapest option comes from PECO and costs less than a fiver.

The actual assembly processes are very simple and you should need little in the way of either tools

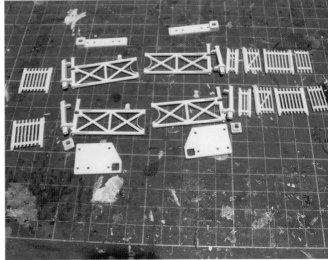

Without all that extra plastic rendering, the PECO version is both more usable and less costly; it also provides a separate pedestrian gate, which is another attractive and useful feature.

or expertise. There is any flash or warping and the only use for the scalpel was to separate the items and remove any pips or mould-lines. The type of polystyrene adhesive you use is up to you: the tube version worked fine for the Dapol and Gaugemaster, while the merest dab of liquid-poly was enough to reinforce the snap-together PECO model. All the instructions are a bit limited, so a dry run in each case is a good idea. All level-crossings are made up of two mirror-image halves and getting these sorted in your mind before you begin sticking things together is sound practice.

All the designs have some good points, as well as some less than helpful ones too, so it is worth looking at each kit in some detail.

Dapol

As might be expected, this is very much a universal or generic model. It is designed to fit the basic train set and could almost be described as a kit rendition of the old die-cast Hornby Dublo version. To be frank, it is hard to see how it might be integrated into a fully scenic layout. The approach ramps are cobbled road, which rather rules them out as sections of the usual tarmac or gravelled highway. The railway crossing itself is all recycled sleepers, which, while suitable for barrow crossings at the ends of platforms, are hardly acceptable for public roads. The sides of the ramps are brickwork, which further emphasizes this

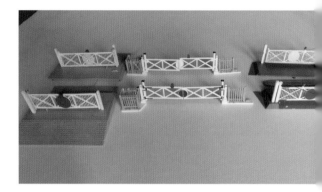

All three kits assembled.

kit's suitability for installation on a table-top train set. The last downside is that the gates lack the mandatory wire-mesh safety fencing, while the red warning lights are certainly unfamiliar-looking!

On the plus side, the kit is inexpensive, goes together very well and the finished model looks fine. As an added bonus, it can be combined into a two-track version and extra parts are included. The missing mesh can be sourced from leftovers from the Ratio Security Fencing or from the Gaugemaster kit if you are using that as well. As an alternative, you could try to scrounge a very small sample of a suitable net from your friendly local curtain shop!

ABOVE, LEFT AND RIGHT: *If the ramps and central portions are to be used, some painting and weathering, both before and after installation, will be needed to blend them into their chosen sites.*

On balance, this version is more appropriate in a station or factory area where road traffic was less frequent and usually less 'weighty'. Paint with enamels or acrylics to match the setting and use pastels to weather it into its surroundings.

Gaugemaster

This is another design that incorporates small ramped sections to lift the vehicular traffic to rail height. In this instance, the road section could be finished as either tarmac or gravel and the flanking sides are grass. The crossing itself is once again sleeper-type with a pre-formed section to sit in the four-foot. There is mesh provided in the pack (enough to do a couple of kits) and the road-facing warning lamp is more subtle. Transverse strengthening wire for the gate is included, but you may want to substitute micro-rod and carry it from the top of the gate-post.

The mouldings are nicely detailed and are complete with relief ironwork to represent the hinges. The ramps and sleepers are still not quite right, but,

at a pinch, you could get away with this model on a single-track branch where it is crossed by a minor road, metalled by-way or urban street. It will all come down to your ability to make it blend in with its surroundings.

PECO

Unlike the last two kits, the PECO is a gates-only pack. Its low cost, and the simple fact that it is designed to fit into an existing road/rail setting, make it more of an aid to the scratch-builder than a stand-alone kit. The main downside is again the lack of the wire-mesh safety fencing, but the upsides are the inclusion of a pair of wicket-gates and a more realistic warning lamp.

Special care needs to be taken with the push-fit gate fixings; try them all in every permutation and be prepared for delicate scalpel work to enlarge the spigot holes. It makes up into a neat little model, but its very simplicity can soon trip up the modeller who is in too much of a hurry.

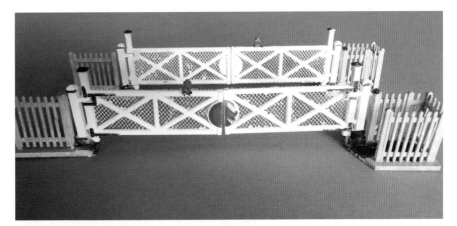

The PECO kit assembled and painted and ready to be installed. It is a bit generously dimensioned for a single-track line and will just about stretch to protect a two-track system.

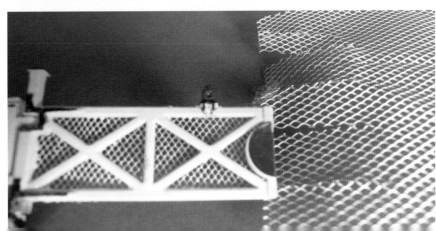

The wire mesh behind the gate's woodwork is an essential element; the item supplied with the Ratio 'Security Fence' kit is acceptable. It would be nice to use real metal mesh, but the finest available is still far too coarse.

'KEEPER'S COTTAGE'

Most rural level-crossings located outside the control of their own signal box were operated by a keeper. This meant that the original companies were usually required to provide some sort of accommodation, however basic. This might take the form of a small two-room cottage, perhaps with the luxury of an outside toilet or garden shed. The site would probably include a vegetable plot and the buildings would be in the company's own style, or that of its Signal & Telegraph contractor. Many of these have now vanished, swept away in the wake of line closures and road improvements, but many were certainly around in the chosen period and therefore merit inclusion.

There is one image that might provide sufficient inspiration and information for a small but appealing scratch-build exercise, but if you want a quicker solu

tion, there are plastic kits available from Springside and Wills Scenics. The latter is a bit basic but it does offer a choice of finishes, while the former has an excellent, almost 'Brunellian' character. If space is limited, then the Springside version is a mere 65 x 56mm (16 x 14ft), while the larger Wills model has a footprint of 98mm (24ft 6in) square. You might also be lucky and find a ready-to-site cottage that is small enough to fulfil the role.

Some keeper's cottages, although not all, could be quite ornate, despite their diminutive size and would therefore make an attractive and justifiable feature on an otherwise fairly bland stretch of line. Just the briefest trawl online revealed everything from two-room wooden shanties to elaborate little two-storey, half-timbered mini-mansions; proving yet again the age-old modeller's maxim that there is 'a prototype for everything'.

'Crossing Keeper's Gothic' – a solidly built and quite substantial cottage for the keeper and his family. The gates would be opened manually, with the signals and locking mechanism housed in the small shed. There would be enough land for a garden and outbuildings, including a primitive toilet. Water would come from a well or pump or by churn on the first train. AUSTIN ATTEWELL

Work is in progress at Dainton Crossing on 'Wessex Lines'; this is the PECO version in situ. No keeper's cottage is needed when the gates are controlled by the signal box.

Assembling the Wills Kit

This is a rather unusual little offering among the vast array of plastic kits, with everything you need contained on pairs of identical sprues. Hence you get a pair of 'front walls', one of which will become the back, and a pair of sides, one of which will become the 'left' while the other will become the 'right'. The roof and chimney stack are likewise each made up of four identical parts. In terms of the manufacturing concept this is very clever idea, using just one set of tooling and letting the modellers decide which way round they will envisage the final result.

This simple little building should have gone together easily, but there are three potential problem areas:

1) On the walls where the four corner joints consist of interlaced stones, A must fit into B, while B must also fit into A. The catch is that they do not. The only solution seems to be a rather tedious hour or so enlarging every recess with a sharp scalpel – all eight corner joints might need this treatment. A final recommendation is to use liquid-poly rather than cement, as this better helps compensate for any final inaccuracies.

2) The second problem arises from the simplicity of the manufacture. The guttering is represented by four identical straight mouldings, with the actual metalwork protruding by two or three millimetres at either end of a wall-length tab. There are no corner mouldings and no provision for any overlap or joints. It is therefore impossible, without some thought and some surgery, to get a properly continuous 'run' of guttering around all four walls. The task is best tackled before the roof is fixed as

RIGHT AND BELOW:
The cottage from Wills Scenics is an attractive and ingenious model, but it does need a bit of attention, including some card or plastic room dividers. The guttering in particular does produce problems at the corners.

The finished Wills model is very pleasing and deserves better than this scrap of 'brownfield' made temporarily available at Winterbourne. It should have a properly detailed plot within which to stand, especially given the potential for the full domestic scene.

this makes for ease of handling and better overall control. To get the actual height right relative to the edge of the roof, each piece should be fixed in line with the bottom of the top course of the stonework. Fix the first full section in place and then keep trimming and trying until you get the best and neatest fit for all four corners. This is definitely a job for the liquid-poly and not the cement tube.

3) The third problem lies with the actual combining of those four quarter-roof sections. They have to join almost seamlessly at the ridges (the ridge tiles should appear to be whole and not two misaligned halves); the corners must be exact right-angles and, last, you have guess whether the joined sections have come out at the correct pitch. This is made trickier by attempting to work the roof and the shell as separate sub-assemblies. If you assemble them in situ on the walls, you may have better luck. It may be possible to disguise any visible gaps or seams on the ridge tiles using liquid-poly to weld sections of small (0.02mm) micro-rod along the full length of ridge. Many real-life ridge tiles do have something similar.

Finishing

The finishing method is entirely up to each modeller and their preferred technique. The usual route involves priming the whole surface with matt white emulsion and then applying washes and individual details with watercolour, before some final weathering with pastel dust. Incidentally, the glazing was cut from the packaging and fixed with Deluxe Glue 'n' Glaze, which seems as good as its reputation suggests. Room partitions and curtains were added to improve the appearance and prevent through-views.

All in all, the Wills cottage is a nice little structure and one that ultimately justifies the necessary extra effort.

It is very reasonably priced and makes an attractive scene especially when included with its crossing-gates, lever frame and a couple of 'stop' signals. Bearing in mind that it is the keeper's family home, there is ample scope for detailing a domestic life too.

If you are able to find sufficient space, do not forget the essential lever frame. This can be portrayed, or even just intimated, by the presence of a shelter. This might be an officially provided little shed or something knocked together by the gate-keeper from sheets of tin or recycled planks. However, many of these frames were open to the elements and you can add some prototypical authenticity by having the frame operated by the keeper's wife.

RIGHT, TOP AND BOTTOM: *The crossings 'works' would often be no more than a simple lever frame, either exposed to the elements or housed in a fairly minimalist structure. These little features were usually stuck in the middle of nowhere, serving a little-used 'B' road crossing a lightly used branch line.*

Level-crossings, large or small, seem tailor-made for scenic cameos. Not all of them carried the Queen's highway; this platform-end version at Winterbourne serves a footpath, a farm access and the station's barrow crossing. It is also a haven for the schoolboy spotters that porter has banned from his platforms!

FINAL CONSIDERATIONS

- All steam-era road/rail crossings should be controlled by a signal box or ground frame.
- The gates must have lever-operated locking mechanisms.
- Most gates should be protected by an appropriate home/stop signal.
- Gates controlled by a signal box will be operated manually by a capstan or electrically powered.

- Gates controlled by a rural lever frame will be physically 'walked' across by the keeper. In this case, you will need a keeper's cottage or at least a hut.
- The railway boundary fence must reach and be secured to the gate-posts.
- The general rule is the gates are open to road traffic unless a train is due. In rural areas it is common to see sharpened timbers alongside the road crossing, to deter livestock.

- Controversially, the reverse looks better on a layout and will help you to run moving trains past stopped traffic! While this is applicable to those with non-operating gates, it is much less relevant to those who run a more automated layout. In that case, it is more than possible to have electrically powered gates, which can, and indeed should, be properly interlocked with their protecting signals. It is sure to be the case that there will be a system somewhere where the road traffic will also move; many continental and US layouts boast a whole host of these automated features and, for anyone aspiring towards the fully computerized model railway, this would be a realistically achievable goal.

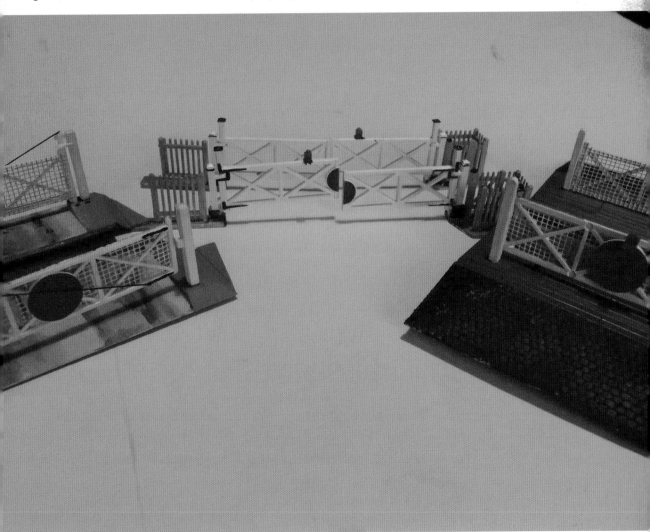

All three kits completed – take your pick.

While Network Rail are being pressured to replace crossings with costly bridges, Swanage Railway have just installed a new one at Norden, which now allows the trains to reach the mainline at Wareham. The controls are housed in the neat little box to the left of the picture.

Three things to note: in the distance is the 'down' home protecting the crossing and the station; next come the two unusual little platforms to facilitate the exchange of the single-line tokens; finally, there is the livestock deterrent created by the timbers laid edge-up on both sides of the roadway.

In the right place at the right time, the camera captures the token exchange with
Scots Guardsman on a steam special en route to Swanage.

CONSTRUCTION METHODS

FORMING CORNERS

SCORE-AND-BEND

Follow the instructions given on the diagram on the opposite page.

BUTT JOINS

When fitting the end/side walls between the front and back ones, they should be shortened twice the thickness of the material. Glue and strengthen them as necessary.

When fitting the front/back walls between the end/side ones, then it is those that should be shortened. This version is recommended for buildings with gable ends.

CHAMFERED JOIN

Proceed as for Option 1, but cut right through and glue/strengthen as necessary (see diagram opposite)..

STRENGTHENING

Use square or triangular strip-wood. Balsa is ideal, being light and easier to work. The 'l' length(s) can be varied to meet your plans for the inside of the building.

Use triangular off-cuts of card; make sure they do not intrude into doors/windows.

Use full area floors, ceilings, bases or false roofs. Expect to use more on taller structures.

FORMING ROOFS

Follow the instructions for forming the roofs of signal boxes that are given on the diagrams on page 234.

Corners

1. Score-and-bend

A. Cut/gouge a 'VEE' as deep as possible-without piercing the outer skin

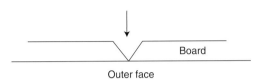

Board

Outer face

B. Carefully bend the next section until you have a sharp corner

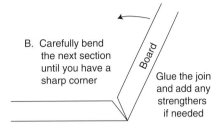

Glue the join and add any strengthers if needed

2. Butt Joins

A

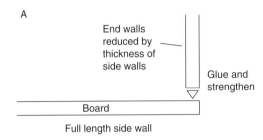

End walls reduced by thickness of side walls

Glue and strengthen

Board

Full length side wall

OR

B

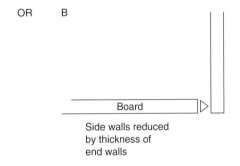

Board

Side walls reduced by thickness of end walls

3. Chamfered join

As for version 1 – but cut right through and glue....

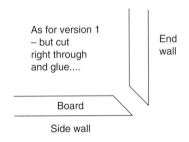

End wall

Board

Side wall

4. 'Strengthers'

a

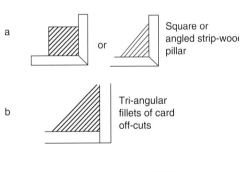

or

Square or angled strip-wood pillar

b

Tri-angular fillets of card off-cuts

c

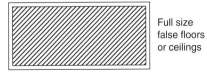

Full size false floors or ceilings

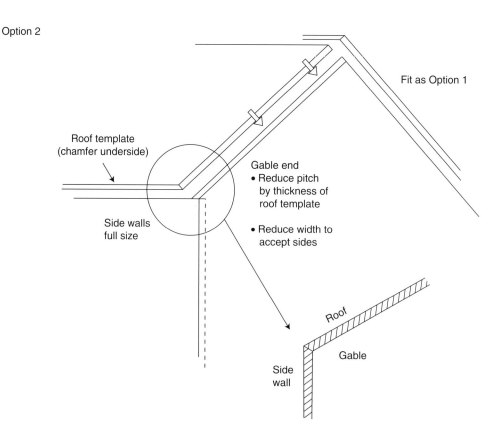

Option 1

Roof
template

Second template
overlaps first
to form
clean ridge

Gable end
(cut full size)

Side walls

(shorten by width
of gable-end card
at both ends)

Roof

Gable

Side
wall

Option 2

Fit as Option 1

Roof template
(chamfer underside)

Gable end
• Reduce pitch
by thickness of
roof template

• Reduce width to
accept sides

Side walls
full size

Roof

Gable

Side
wall

BASIC SIGNALS/SIGNALLING FOR LAYOUTS

The following diagrams are in no way intended to be perfect examples of signalling, but an excuse to include a plentiful array of signal types within a small area, at the same time, ensuring that each one is appropriate for its allotted role.

Note that starting signals are often mounted on shorter posts, and are frequently sited very close to the platform ends or even on the actual platforms. Distant signals have been deliberately omitted from the more simple diagrams.

The diagrams are to be found on page 236.

Typical signals/signalling for layouts

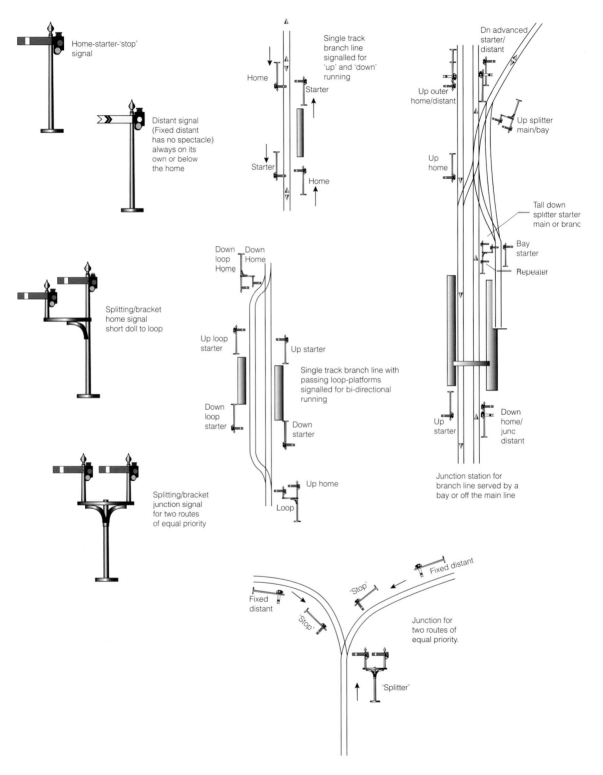

Home-starter-'stop' signal

Distant signal (Fixed distant has no spectacle) always on its own or below the home

Splitting/bracket home signal short doll to loop

Splitting/bracket junction signal for two routes of equal priority

Single track branch line signalled for 'up' and 'down' running

Home

Starter

Starter

Home

Down loop Home

Down Home

Up loop starter

Up starter

Single track branch line with passing loop-platforms signalled for bi-directional running

Down loop starter

Down starter

Up home

Loop

Dn advanced starter/ distant

Up outer home/distant

Up splitter main/bay

Up home

Tall down splitter starter main or branc

Bay starter

Repeater

Up starter

Down home/ junc distant

Junction station for branch line served by a bay or off the main line

Fixed distant

Fixed distant

'Stop'

'Stop'

Junction for two routes of equal priority.

'Splitter'

RECOMMENDED READING AND RESOURCES

INSPIRATION AND INFORMATION

There is plenty of information available, whether you want to delve deeply into a prototype, and have a commitment to a particular period, company, region or general locality, or you are simply searching for some inspiration. Browsing through any steam album, or the relevant magazines such as will provide the latter. Online, two of the most useful websites are signalbox.org and geograph.org.uk.

For those newer to modelling, there is no shortage of advice available. The main 'big three' magazines are an obvious choice, as is your local dealership, where you should expect to receive accurate and impartial help. There is also the wonderful world of the web, where you can while away your precious modelling time on the keyboard rather than on the layout!

MAGAZINES

Steam Days
Steam World
British Railways Illustrated,
The 'Big Three': *Railway Modeller, Model Rail, British Railway Modelling*

BOOKS

Gasson, Harold *Signalling Days*, OPC 0 86093 118 8
Jackson, Allen *A Contemporary Perspective on GWR Signalling*, The Crowood Press 978 1 84797 950 6
Rhodes, Michael *Re-Signalling Britain*, Moretons Media 978 1 909128 64 4
Rice, Ian *Railway Modelling the Realistic Way*, Haynes 978 1 84425 359 3
Simmons, Norman *Railway Modelling*, PSL 0 85059 557 6
Vaughan, Adrian *Glory Days of a Western Signal Man*, Ian Allan 0 7110 2715 3

Vaughan, Adrian *The Heart of the Great Western*, Silver Link 1 85794 026 1
Vaughan, Adrian *A Pictorial Record of Great Western Signalling*, OPC 0902888 08 0
Vaughan, Adrian *Railways Through the Vale of The White Horse*, The Crowood Press 978 1 84797 871 4

RESOURCES

Much of what has been used in this book, and indeed on all my layouts, is widely available from local dealerships, exhibitions, toy fairs or hobby shops. Many of the more specialized items can be obtained by mail order or by shopping via the appropriate websites. These are easy to locate from the advertisement pages in the magazines or from a quick online search.

The following list of sources for downloads and laser-cut products may be helpful, but remember that ranges and availability change all the time, so you will need check first.

DOWNLOADS

scalescenes.com
smartmodels.com
hall-royd-junction.co.uk
scalemodelscenery.co.uk
railwayscenics.com
[b head] Laser-Cut Kits
timbertracks.co.uk
osbornsmodels.com
4trackmodels.co.uk
yorkmodelmaking.co.uk

OTHERS

springsidemodels.com
Alphagraphix, 23 Darris Road, Selly Park, Birmingham, B29 7QY
freestonemodel.co.uk

INDEX

RELATED TITLES FROM CROWOOD

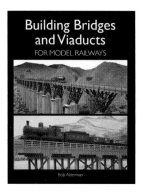

Building Bridges and Viaducts for Model Railways
BOB ALDERMAN
ISBN 978 1 84797 818 9
500 illustrations, 192pp

Modelling Ports and Inland Waterways – A Guide for Railway Modellers
DAVID WRIGHT
ISBN 978 1 78500 167 3
390 illustrations, 192pp

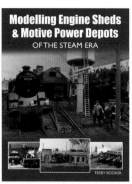

Modelling Engine Sheds and Motive Power Depots of the Steam Era
TERRY BOOKER
ISBN 978 1 78500 114 7
320 illustrations, 208pp

Modelling the Lineside
RICHARD BARDSLEY
ISBN 978 1 78500 139 0
240 illustrations, 160pp

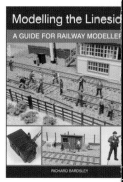

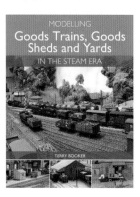

Modelling Goods Trains, Goods Sheds and Yards in the Steam Era
TERRY BOOKER
ISBN 978 1 78500 068 3
245 illustrations, 192pp

Modelling Railway Stations
IAN LAMB
ISBN 978 1 84797 951 3
200 illustrations, 176pp

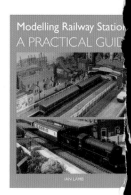

In case of difficulty ordering, please contact the Sales Office:

The Crowood Press
Ramsbury
Wiltshire
SN8 2HR
UK

Tel: 44 (0) 1672 520320
enquiries@crowood.com
www.crowood.com